HOSTAGE!

L.B. TAYLOR, JR.

KIDNAPPING AND TERRORISM IN OUR TIME

Franklin Watts
New York / London / Toronto / Sydney / 1989
An Impact Book

51853

Photographs courtesy of:
Reuters/Bettmann Newsphotos: pp. 13, 26, 54, 72 (both);
UPI/Bettmann Newsphotos: pp. 41, 59 (top), 81, 92;
Gamma-Liaison: pp. 18 (Jerome Chatin), 29 (Eric
Bouvet), 48 (Simon Urli), 59 (bottom) and 62 (Alain
Mingam), 67 (P. Aventurier), 105 (Patrick Piel); Bett-
mann Archive: p. 34; AP/Wide World Photos: p. 101.

Library of Congress Cataloging-in-Publication Data
Taylor, L. B.
Hostage! : kidnapping and terrorism in our time / by L. B. Taylor, Jr.
p.   cm.—(Impact)
Bibliography: p.
Includes index.
Summary: Discusses terrorism and hostage-taking as major problems
in the world today, their effects on how we live, and the methods
employed to reduce terrorism.
ISBN 0-531-10661-6
1. Terrorism—Juvenile literature.   2. Kidnapping—Juvenile
literature. [1. Terrorism. 2. Kidnapping. 3. Hostages.]
I. Title.
HV6431.T418   1989
364.1'54—dc20   89-5828   CIP   AC

CONTENTS

HOSTAGE!

CHAPTER ONE

TERROR AT SEA

In looking back on it, suspicion should have been aroused when the four swarthy young men boarded the luxury cruise ship *Achille Lauro* at Genoa, Italy, on October 3, 1985. Most of the other 744 passengers were middle-aged or elderly tourists.

The on-board behavior of the four young men was suspicious, too. They stayed in their cabin as the ship sailed first to Naples, then to Syracuse, and finally to Alexandria, Egypt. They ate all their meals in their cramped room, and when they did venture outside, they carried attaché cases.

At Alexandria, 650 of the passengers disembarked to go on an excursion to see the great pyramids. The *Achille Lauro* then slowly moved eastward along the coast toward Port Said, where it was to reboard the sightseers. At lunchtime, a waiter on the ship entered the cabin of the four men and found them cleaning an awesome arsenal of automatic weapons. This discovery forced the group to act before they were ready.

They were Arab terrorists, and their mission was to hijack the cruise ship and hold its passengers and crew hostage. For the next few minutes, the four men seemed to go mad. They ran through the corridors of the ship spraying the walls with bullets.

Most of the passengers left on board were in the dining room for the noon meal. They were ordered to lie on the floor, and those who had finished eating were told to return to the dining room. One woman, who had a foot amputated and walked slowly with a cane, apparently didn't move fast enough for the terrorists. They kicked her down a staircase.

Stark fear spread among those lying face-down in the dining room, as the terrorists ran about screaming in a language few understood. Then they searched through everyone's passport. They singled out fourteen Americans, six Britons, and two Austrians and herded them into another, smaller room, where the hostages were forced to sit next to cans of gasoline.

There, the Arabs played deadly "games" with the frightened passengers. Periodically, they sprayed bullets into the walls over the heads of the twenty-two. Then they pulled the pins from hand grenades and made three women sit and hold the live weapons. All of the hostages were seated close together, so that if the women lost their grip, everyone would have been blown up.

Meanwhile, the ship's captain, who had walked down from the bridge to see what was going on, was ordered back to the bridge. There, two of the four terrorists aimed machine guns at him, occasionally firing random shots at the ground. They told the captain to sail the ship to Tartus, a Syrian port just north of Lebanon. With guns at his back, the captain followed orders through the long, tense night.

The next day, in the waters just off Tartus, the hijackers made their demands known. They wanted an international diplomatic team assembled to hear them out. They had two conditions. One, they wanted fifty Palestinian prisoners being held in Israel to be freed. Two, they wanted safe-conduct to leave the ship and escape to Syria. By now much of the world was following via television the grisly drama being played out.

Problems arose when the Syrian authorities didn't respond quickly enough to the demands. The terrorists threatened to begin killing the passengers. Then they acted. They singled out a sixty-nine-year-old man named Leon Klinghoffer, who was confined to a wheelchair. Apparently he had been chosen for two reasons—he was American and he was Jewish.

Despite the protests of Klinghoffer's wife, they wheeled the crippled man to the edge of the ship's rail. And there, in cold blood, one of the terrorists opened fire with his automatic rifle at point-blank range, killing Klinghoffer instantly. The Arabs then had him and his wheelchair thrown overboard.

The terrorists reentered the ship's bridge and told the startled captain, "We have just killed a man." They then picked up the ship-to-shore radio and boasted, "We threw the first body into the water after shooting him in the head. Minutes from now, we will follow up with the second one."

But the Syrians surprised them. "Go back where you came from," an official said. Perplexed, the terrorists ordered the captain to sail toward Beirut.

For the next day or so, life aboard the *Achille Lauro* was a nightmare of confusion and horror. When the Lebanese refused the terrorists' demands, the captain was ordered to turn toward Libya; then the course was altered again. Aboard ship, the passengers feared for their lives as the Arabs ran about indiscriminately hitting and kicking people and striking them with their rifles.

Two days after they had taken over the ship, the Arabs made contact with Egypt. By now, realizing that their demands to free Palestinian prisoners were not going to be met, they said they would free the hostages and leave the ship if Egypt would guarantee them safe-conduct into the hands of the Palestine Liberation Organization (PLO), to which they belonged.

Egyptian authorities, declaring that their only motive was to save others from being killed, granted the request. Two PLO men took a harbor boat out to the *Achille Lauro* and picked up the hijackers, who left the ship waving in triumph. The six men then returned to shore and were driven to an airport, where they boarded an Egyptian airliner sometime later and took off for a flight out of the country.

When the terrorists left the ship, it foiled a plan U.S. military forces had been working on that called for an assault force to storm the *Achille Lauro* at sea. But as the Egyptian airliner took off, a second plan was quickly put into operation. Four U.S. F-14 Tomcat fighter-interceptors were launched from the aircraft carrier *Saratoga*. In less than two hours, they pulled alongside the airliner, which was apparently headed for Tunis. The Egyptian pilot asked for permission to land in Tunis but was refused. He then tried to land in Athens, Greece, but was denied entry there, too.

Then the U.S. fighters dipped their wings in the international signal for a forced landing. The plane landed at the U.S. Sigonella Naval Air Base in Sicily. Once on the ground, the four Arab hijackers were soon apprehended by Italian authorities and taken into custody.

This daring conclusion to a harrowing episode was widely applauded by U.S. officials and the public, who for years had watched, virtually helpless, as terrorists held Americans hostage at foreign sites around the world, from Tehran to Beirut. Said U.S. Senator Robert Byrd of West Virginia: "Finally, we have changed the rules. We have shown the world that the United States

*The Italian cruise ship
Achille Lauro, surrounded by
smaller vessels five days
after the ship was hijacked by
Palestinian gunmen*

is a force to be reckoned with in the global battle against terrorist actions."

At a Washington news conference, President Ronald W. Reagan said that terrorists had at last been put on notice that "you can run but you can't hide. . . . What we want is justice done."[1]

CHAPTER TWO

A MOST
EFFECTIVE WEAPON

Although the *Achille Lauro* hijackers were captured without achieving their demands, the success of the U.S. mission to bring the terrorists to justice offers no long-term solution to the continuing problem of hostage-taking around the world. And even the *Achille Lauro* success had its critics. Many around the world viewed the U.S. action in overtaking the Egyptian airliner as an act of piracy in international airspace. In addition, some experts contended that had the United States landed an assault team on the ship while the hijackers were still aboard, as originally planned, many of the unarmed passengers and crew members might have been killed before the terrorists could have been stopped. Finally, U.S. relations with Egypt were severely strained because Egyptian president Hosni Mubarak had given his word to the Palestinians that they would receive safe passage out of his country. Mubarak claimed he had lost credibility with the PLO.

Although the use of military force had worked in this case, there are many instances of hostage-taking where it cannot be effectively applied. Thus, despite this one success, the problem still looms large, and there appears to be no simple answer to it.

Moreover, the capture of the four Arab hijackers did not seem to have any lasting effect as a deterrent to further instances of hostage-taking. For the fact is that this type of insidious crime—the holding of human beings against their will for various forms of ransom—has become one of the most effective weapons in the terrorists' arsenal.

Hostage-taking has become a sign of our times. It is a major international problem that occurs in countries all over the world. It has spread from South America in the late 1960s and early 1970s to Europe, the Middle East, and North America in the 1980s. During this time, there have been thousands of instances of hostage-taking by individuals and by fanatical groups.

Terrorists take hostages for several reasons. They know they can get worldwide media exposure and command millions of dollars in ransom. And they know they can publicly embarrass national governments in the process.

This point was proven most dramatically from 1979 to 1981 when youthful Iranian revolutionaries held more than fifty Americans hostage in Iran for 444 days. The United States, the most powerful nation in the free world, was held virtually helpless during this humiliating period.

Consider that between 1970 and 1977, says Caroline Moorehead in her book *Hostages to Fortune,* terrorist movements throughout the world kidnapped more than three hundred people. These actions resulted in ransom payoffs of more than $160 million and the release of nearly three hundred political prisoners. It also brought widespread publicity for radical groups. As Moorehead points out, no one knew much about the Baader-Meinhof gang, the Palestinians, or the South Moluccans until their criminal exploits began to fill the newspapers and television screens day after day.

For statistical proof that kidnapping is an effective tool, the U.S. State Department's Office for the Combatting of Terrorism reports that between the years 1968 and 1982, there were more than 400 incidents of hostage-taking involving 950 victims. The kidnappers escaped with their hostages more than 80 percent of the time and collected ransoms in more than 70 percent of the cases in which ransoms were demanded. It has been estimated that during this period terrorists were paid ransoms totaling $350 million, with U.S.-based corporations alone paying in excess of $150 million.

The United States is not the only victim. Such countries as the Soviet Union, West Germany, Great Britain, and Israel have been totally frustrated in trying to deal with hostage situations involving their citizens and government officials. As we saw in the United States during the Reagan administration, even where there is supposedly a set policy, the rules are often broken. President Reagan, for example, long proclaimed that the United States would never give in to terrorist demands even at the expense of hostages' lives. Yet, as Americans learned in 1987, the U.S. government secretly sent arms to Iran in exchange for that country's help in freeing U.S. hostages being held in Lebanon.

Hostage-taking has changed the way we live, too. Business executives and government officials based in foreign countries, for example, today often employ bodyguards. They have bulletproof cars and take several different routes to work in an effort to foil terrorists who may be tracking them.

At airports around the world today, one must pass through sophisticated metal-detection devices, used as a deterrent to skyjackings, which were so common a few years ago. At many airports around the world, armed guards stand on alert.

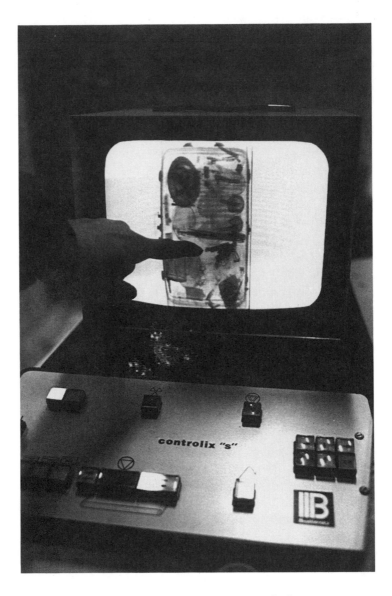

*Modern airport security includes
metal detection devices, such as this
one, for locating guns hidden in hand
luggage carried aboard a plane.*

After a number of skyjackings and the taking of the *Achille Lauro,* tens of thousands of American tourists canceled vacations to Europe and the Middle East. Hostage-taking generates great fear among people. The very threat of being held by hostile captors has caused many to change their plans.

And, of course, hostage-taking has caused deep psychological problems for those who have been victims of it. It has caused great mental anguish and lingering terror that sometimes has taken months or years to get over. It leaves scars on the families of hostages as well.

The dilemma of hostage-taking looms as large today as it did twenty years ago, when terrorists first began applying this tactic. The solution to it is still to be found.

CHAPTER THREE

PROFILE OF
TERRORISM

What exactly is terrorism, and who are today's terrorists? In 1980, the Central Intelligence Agency (CIA) offered this definition: "The threat or use of violence for political purposes by individuals or groups, whether acting for or in opposition to established governmental authority, when such actions are intended to shock, stun, or intimidate a target group wider than the immediate victims. Terrorism has involved groups seeking to overthrow specific regimes, to rectify perceived national or group grievances, or to undermine international order as an end in itself."[2]

But, as some have pointed out, such a broad definition is not totally acceptable because it unintentionally includes other, nonterrorist, activities such as guerrilla warfare. Walter Laqueur, author of *The Age of Terrorism,* says that guerrilla warfare is often confused with terrorism. Guerrilla warfare has the goal of establishing liberated areas in the countryside and setting up small military units that will gradually grow in strength and number, from squads, companies, and regiments into divisions and armies. In liberated areas, Laqueur says, guerrillas establish their own institutions, conduct propaganda, and engage in other open political activities. None of this, he points out, applies to terrorists, whose base of operation is in the cities and who have to operate clandestinely in small units.[3]

Commandos differ from terrorists, also, in that they are generally members of an organized military unit specially trained for hit-and-run raids into enemy territory. Insurgents are distinguished from terrorists in that they are usually engaged in a loosely organized revolt against a ruling government.

Part of the aim of a terrorist group, says James Adams, author of *The Financing of Terror*, is to commit acts of such barbarity (including hostage-taking) that they will provoke the government they oppose into acts of repression, such as house-to-house searches, imprisonment without trial, or the passing of laws that restrict freedom. These acts generally win recruits to the terrorists' cause and may allow the terrorists to "graduate" to guerrilla warfare. Adams also says that in trying to provoke that type of repressive reaction, terrorists typically will treat civilians as legitimate targets, whereas guerrillas, relying as they do on a broader political base, tend to concentrate more on military targets as they push a country toward civil war.

Adams has thus come up with his own definition of terrorism. He says that, "A terrorist is an individual or member of a group that wishes to achieve political ends using violent means, often at the cost of casualties to innocent civilians and with the support of only a minority of the people they represent."[4]

In the Public Report of Vice-President George Bush's Task Force on Combatting Terrorism, published in February 1986, terrorism is defined as: "The unlawful use or threat of violence against persons or property to further political or social objectives. It is usually intended to intimidate or coerce a government, individuals, or groups, or to modify their behavior or politics."[5]

Can we draw a clear profile of today's terrorists? There are a few common denominators. For one thing, most of them are young, and a large number are students. Says the Bush report: "Fully 60 percent of the Third World population is under 20 years of age; half are 15 years or less. These population pressures create a volatile mixture of youthful aspirations that, when coupled with economic and political frustrations, help form a large pool of potential terrorists."[6]

To this point, Laqueur adds: "That their [terrorist-group] members have been young is the only feature common to all terrorist movements. Sometimes 30 is considered almost elderly. The overwhelming majority of active terrorists are in their 20s, and there has been a tendency, in particular among Arab and Iranian groups, to use boys aged 14 and 15 for dangerous missions, partly perhaps because they are less likely to question instructions, but also because they are less likely to attract attention."[7]

Terrorists also are zealously dedicated. The Bush report states, "Many terrorists have a deep belief in the justice of their cause. They are rough and vicious and may have little regard for their own lives or those of their victims in attempting to achieve their goals. Others may even be hired assassins [or kidnappers]."[8]

Experts are in general agreement that most terrorists are fanatics, and that fanaticism often makes for cruelty. Ordinary criminals have usually shown greater humanity than terrorists, probably because most of them are out for profit and not for psychological satisfaction. Terrorists commonly kill in cold blood and torture their victims, either physically, psychologically, or both. Many hostages, for example, have been held in solitary confinement for long periods of time, constantly harassed, and, in some instances, even buried alive.

Beyond this, there are few common characteristics. Some terrorists had unhappy childhoods and were dirt-poor. But others came from solid middle-class homes. Women seem to be as dedicated to their cause as men, and minorities are prominently represented. Politically, terrorists have represented the extremes of both the left and right spectrums (liberal and conservative). Some have been members of national and religious groups; others have acted totally independently.

Their groups are generally small, often consisting of from three to ten people, as is common today among terrorists operating in Lebanon. Some groups number in the dozens, and a few, historically, reached up to a few thousand in size, although the larger the group's size, the easier it is to track its members.

According to the Bush report, there are two basic categories of terrorists today. One includes those who are self-supported. These rely primarily on their own initiatives, such as extortion, hostage-taking, bank robberies, and narcotics trafficking, to support their activities. Such groups tend to be extremely security conscious, keeping their numbers small to avoid penetration efforts.

On the other hand, state-sponsored or state-aided terrorist groups are frequently larger in number, have the advantage of protection by state agencies, and are able to use state intelligence resources in planning and carrying out their activities. They are subject to some control by their sponsors and may be expected to carry out attacks for them. Because of the haven provided by the host country and the compartmentalized operations of terrorist organizations, it is extremely difficult to penetrate such groups.[9]

The U.S. government believes state-supported terrorists are substantially more dangerous than those operating independently. L. Paul Bremer, III, U.S. ambassador at large for counterterrorism, claims that state sponsorship gives clear advantages to the terrorist. He summarizes these advantages as follows:

- When a terrorist obtains legitimate travel and identification documents from a patron state, it becomes harder to identify and track him or her.

- A state-supported terrorist has a ready source of weapons and a ready means to transport them. By international convention, embassies are exempt from search, and the baggage handlers at state-owned airlines comply when directed not to examine a particular parcel.

- Countries such as Libya, Syria, and Iran make a terrorist's work easier by providing a place for training.

- The refuge supplied by patron states in itself constitutes important support. Being able to live without fear of immediate arrest and punishment is of enormous psychological value to a terrorist.

- Finally, financial support from state sponsors allows terrorists to spend more time on operations because they need not rob banks or traffic in drugs to raise money.

Why do certain countries sponsor terrorists? Bremer, in a special report to Congress in October 1987, cited several reasons. "Terrorism," he said, "can be an inexpensive form of warfare. A small group of terrorists costs less per year than a company of regular soldiers and can cause far more havoc in an enemy state than could that company of soldiers.

"Using terrorists makes it easier for the sponsoring state to deny responsibility for actions which, if taken overtly, could lead to war. A state can also use terrorists to murder [or kidnap] dissidents abroad."[10]

Although there are far too many different terrorist groups operating in the world today to name them all, a few have gained considerable notoriety in the past decade. Among the most prominent groups operating out of Lebanon currently is one generally known as Hezbollah, a faction of what is known as the Islamic Jihad. Experts believe the Jihad, which is supported by Iran, has been responsible for almost all of the kidnappings of Westerners in Lebanon in the mid- to late 1980s. In fact, there is considerable evidence to support the claim that Iran exercises strong influence over all hostage-related decisions. "For example," Bremer says, "we [the United States] believe Iran ordered the June 1987 kidnapping of journalist Charles Glass, who was held for two months before he escaped in August."[11]

Other leading terrorist groups have been made up of members of different segments of militant Lebanese Shiites, from the Shia branch of Islam. Religious radicals in this sect are believed to be under the control of the Iranian and Syrian governments. One branch, the Al Jihad al Islami, became known in the mid-1980s for its vicious attacks against U.S. marines in Lebanon, and for the skyjacking of international airliners and the subsequent taking of hostages, including many Americans.

Still another dominant terrorist group has been led by Palestinian leader Abu Nidal, described by experts as ruthless. This unit was supported for a time by Libya and later by Syria, helping its members to gain note as hired terrorists, killers, and kidnappers.

These are only a few of the better-known terrorist groups operating today. There are many others, and more are developing today in the fertile spawning grounds of war-torn Lebanon and in other areas of the world where strife and injustice rule.

Over the past three decades there have been some major geographical shifts in the distribution of international terrorist incidents. In the late 1950s and 1960s, for

Palestinian terrorist Abu Nidal.
This picture was taken in Beirut in 1982.

example, the great majority of kidnappings, killings, bombings, and other activities occurred in South America, principally in Argentina, Brazil, and Uruguay.

In the 1970s, as tough, military-led governments crushed terrorist movements in South America, new groups emerged halfway around the world, and suddenly Western Europe became the prime target. West Germany and Italy were especially hard hit during this period.

In the 1980s, after stiffer national policies and stronger enforcement of them reduced the number of incidents in Europe, the terrorist emphasis moved once again, this time to the Middle East. Throughout the 1980s and still today, the number-one hot spot is Lebanon. Nearly half of all terrorist raids, and an even greater number of hostage-takings, occur in this troubled part of the world.

However, many terrorist organizations have continued to operate in Europe, including the Italian Red Brigades, the French Direct Action, the German Red Army Faction, and the Provisional Irish Republican Army. Additionally, campaigns of fear have been waged in Spain, Portugal, and Greece. Roughly one-fourth of all terrorist attacks in the 1980s have taken place in Europe.

During this period, continuing social, economic, and political turmoil have resulted in cementing existing patterns of insurgency as well as international and domestic terrorism in several Latin American countries, particularly in El Salvador, Colombia, Guatemala, Chile, and Peru. Nicaragua and Cuba also have been implicated in various attacks in the region, which has accounted for approximately 16 percent of all terrorist activities this decade.

Surprisingly, less than 1 percent of such activities take place in the United States. Nevertheless, terrorism deeply troubles the American people. A Roper poll conducted in 1985 showed that 78 percent of all Americans considered terrorism to be one of the most serious current problems facing the United States government, along with the deficit, strategic-arms control, and unemployment.[12]

More recently, in the late 1980s, terrorism has moved into Asia. One of the newer hotbed target areas is Pakistan. In the past several years, there has been a rising number of bombings, assassinations, and attempted kidnappings in Karachi and other major Pakistani cities as well as in the mountainous provinces.

This brand of terrorism, according to U.S. intelligence sources, is backed by the Soviet Union and actually began to operate in the early 1980s, escalating into major incidents in recent years. In fact, in the past two years Pakistan accounted for 45 percent of all those killed or wounded in terrorist bombings.

The reason behind this vicious campaign is that Pakistan has harbored both refugees and guerrilla fighters from neighboring Afghanistan. The Soviet Union and Afghanistan waged a bitter war during most of this decade, and the Soviets launched their attacks in an effort to put pressure on Pakistan to stop allowing Afghanis access to its borders.

Although the Soviet Union has supplied the money, arms, and training for this reign of terror, it has also used Afghan rebels to carry out the deadly missions. It is estimated that there are more than 3 million Afghan refugees and fugitives in Pakistan, but the bombings have mostly killed innocent civilians not involved in the political dispute.

There was also evidence in mid-1988 that, even though the Soviets were pulling their troops out of Afghanistan, they were still planning to continue to fight. Asian intelligence sources have reported that the

An Afghanistan rebel on guard duty

Soviet Union was training terrorists to handle high-tech weapons, including surface-to-air missiles and ground-to-ground missiles. These, it was reported, were intended to be used against aircraft, Afghan refugee camps, and other ground installations.

From the Soviet standpoint, the terrorist campaign has worked in that it has fueled growing Pakistani resentment of the Afghan refugees and anger at the Pakistani government for failing to protect its own citizens, and it has brought pressure on Afghan leaders to speed a settlement to the war. There has been practically nothing the Pakistanis could do in response to the attacks. When the Soviets bombed the country earlier, Pakistan had asked for and gotten aid from the United States, but as one Pakistani official put it, "What do you ask for to combat this kind of terrorism?"[13]

Who have been the major targets of terrorists in the 1980s? Half of the worldwide incidents in the decade have been aimed at only ten countries: eight European nations, Israel, and the United States. In fact, fully one-third of terrorist activities have been strikes at U.S. interests abroad.

Overall, the number of terrorist acts has generally risen since official statistics were first compiled in 1968, with a trend toward bloodier incidents with more fatalities. Attacks caused only twenty deaths in 1968, compared to 926 in 1985.

According to the Public Report of the Vice-President's Task Force on Combatting Terrorism, incidents in the mid-1980s clearly "demonstrated that terrorism is increasingly directed against the Western democracies. The June 14, 1985, skyjacking of TWA Flight 847 shortly after it left Athens, Greece, was the first skyjacking of a U.S. airliner in the Middle East since 1970. In addition, the skyjackings of Egyptair Flight 648 and the *Achille Lauro* cruise ship, the bombings on the outskirts of Madrid of a restaurant frequented by American servicemen, and the shooting of the off-duty Marine Corps personnel in El Salvador demonstrated that Americans are being specifically targeted."[14]

The report also cites that during the 1980s, terrorists have attacked U.S. officials or installations abroad approximately once every seventeen days. In the past twenty years, terrorists have killed or kidnapped as many U.S. diplomats as were killed or kidnapped in the previous 180 years.

CHAPTER FOUR

A HISTORY OF
HOSTAGE-TAKING

Hostage-taking and kidnapping may be as old as civilization itself. There are numerous references to abductions throughout Greek mythology. The great Roman emperor Julius Caesar was captured in 78 B.C. by pirates and held for a fortune in ransom. In medieval times, marauding tribes took hostages for money or for safe passage home. During the Crusades, some enterprising kings made considerable fortunes by ransoming prisoners. In the year 1192, King Richard I of England was captured by Duke Leopold of Austria and held for 150,000 marks of silver. It took the entire wool crop of two religious orders and the levying of special taxes to secure the king's safe return.

In fact, things got so bad from the twelfth through the sixteenth centuries that traveling kings and emperors took hostages themselves to guarantee their own safe passage through foreign lands. Other leaders and prominent citizens often traveled in disguise and had "stand-ins" to take their place if they were captured.

In those days, even if one was held against his or her

will, life was not all that bad. Captors were expected to treat their hostages more as guests than prisoners. And in medieval England, a common practice among those whose estates were in financial trouble was to marry rich heiresses. If the heiress was unwilling, she was simply abducted.

In Europe, highway bandits also used the technique of kidnapping to procure funds, particularly from the sixteenth to eighteenth century. In Italy, such tactics were used for hundreds of years, dating back to Roman times. Even today, it is considered unsafe to travel in the remote mountains of Sardinia. Italian bandits were frequently ruthless, and their negotiations with the hostages' families were gruesomely effective when they displayed a severed ear or finger of the victim.

Part of the swashbuckling lore of the Barbary pirates included kidnapping as a way of making money. Between the fifteenth and eighteenth centuries, there was a steady business of trading captives back and forth across the Mediterranean Sea. Algerian pirates once took 4,000 prisoners from the kingdom of Granada in one raid alone. Algiers was a pirate stronghold for centuries, dating back to the Middle Ages, when the notorious Barbarossa terrorized the entire region. He once returned to the city with 5,000 captives from Minorca, and on another occasion he raided the Adriatic coast, kidnapping 2,500 children from prominent Venetian families.[15] In the latter part of the seventeenth century and throughout the eighteenth, countless thousands of Africans—men, women, boys, and girls—were snatched from their native homeland, chained, and then sailed across the Atlantic Ocean to be sold as slaves to American colonists.

In the 1920s and 1930s, a great outbreak of kidnappings took place on the other side of the world, in China. The victims were missionaries and diplomats who were held for ransoms of money, drugs, and even clothing.

The Barbary Coast pirates

Probably the most famous kidnapping of all time occurred on the night of March 1, 1932, when the infant son of the American pilot-hero Charles Lindbergh, Jr., was taken from his home in New Jersey. The crime captured the attention of the entire country, and the largest manhunt in history searched in vain for the missing child. He was found dead two months later. Sometime afterward, a man named Bruno Hauptmann was charged with the abduction, tried, found guilty, and executed.

This incident dramatized how vulnerable children were and are as hostages. And it was during this same period in the early 1930s that a virtual epidemic of child kidnappings broke out. Dozens of children were taken, and millions of dollars in ransoms were paid out for their return.

A decade later, halfway around the world in Europe, a different form of mass abduction took place. In this case, starting in 1940, thousands of tall, fair-haired, and blue-eyed children from such countries as Denmark, Norway, Holland, Hungary, and Poland were taken from their parents and brought to Germany. This was part of Adolf Hitler's master plan to create a "superrace" of Aryan people by having the children raised and eventually mated together. Many of these young people stayed in Germany after World War II ended. Most of them had been six years old or younger when they were taken and had only dim memories of their birth families and native lands.

The practice of hostage-taking as a terrorist tactic for political purposes is, with a few historical exceptions, a relatively new development. It has evolved as a widespread activity only over the past twenty or so years. And, although the vast majority of hostage incidents have taken place in Europe and the Middle East, especially in recent years, the roots can be found in South America.

It was in Brazil in the 1960s that the young revolutionary Carlos Marighella, greatly disturbed to see his country becoming a police state, wrote what has become the textbook of terrorists worldwide. It is entitled *Mini-Manual for Urban Guerrillas*, and it strongly advocates that groups with grievances should use such criminal actions as bombings, shootings, and kidnappings to achieve their objectives.

Marighella believed that the more terrifying the act, the greater the attention it would command, allowing the terrorists to air their grievances to widespread, if horrified, audiences. Thus, if innocent people were killed, or important government officials or prominent business people were taken hostage, these deeds would rate large headlines and result in lengthy television coverage.

Marighella showed uncommon foresight when he wrote specifically about hostage-taking. "Kidnapping," he said, "is capturing and holding in a secret spot a police agent, a North American spy, a political personality or a notorious enemy of the revolutionary movement. Kidnapping is used to exchange or liberate imprisoned revolutionary comrades, or to force the suspension of torture in the jail cells of the military dictatorship.

"The kidnapping of personalities who are known artists, sports figures, or are outstanding in some other field, but who have evidenced no political interest, can be a useful form of propaganda for the revolutionary and patriotic principles of the urban guerrilla, provided it occurs under special circumstances, and is handled so that the public sympathizes with it and accepts it.

"The kidnapping of North American residents or visitors in Brazil constitutes a form of protest against penetration and domination of United States imperialism in our country."[16]

Radical groups in Brazil and in other countries around the world quickly adopted Marighella's book as their operational bible. Up to this time, terrorists had used bombings as their main weapon, but this had triggered murderous reprisals and massive jailings instead of the intended goals of public sympathy for the overthrowing of governments they considered unfair. Now, revolutionary groups turned to hostage-taking.

It turned out to be a much more effective, and relatively safer, weapon. The act itself is efficient. It ties up few terrorists, yet creates a widespread feeling of insecurity. It doesn't require the use of sophisticated weapons. Best of all, its impact is generally greater than the deed itself, largely through the international publicity it engenders.

The first significant hostage to be captured was Charles Elbrick, the U.S. ambassador to Brazil. Returning to the U.S. embassy in Rio de Janeiro on a September afternoon in 1969 after lunch, his official car stopped before a stalled vehicle. Four men, each carrying pistols, grabbed Elbrick and took him, blindfolded, to a suburban house. There, for three days, he was held in a small, bare room furnished only with a stool and a cot.

His captors told him they were members of MR-8, the Communist party's student faction. They sent a three-page letter, listing their demands, to the U.S. embassy in Rio. In it, the students wrote: "We would like to warn all those who torture, beat, and kill our comrades that we will no longer allow this to continue." They demanded the release of fifteen political prisoners being held by Brazilian police. They also said they wanted the letter read over the national radio. Failure to carry out their instructions, they warned, would lead to Elbrick's execution.

The kidnapping attracted immediate attention, both in Brazil and around the world. The U.S. government exerted heavy pressure on Brazilian leaders to comply with the demands. The prisoners were freed and flown to safety in Mexico. Once the kidnappers got word of this, they released the ambassador unharmed.[17]

The Elbrick episode had widespread implications and set a dangerous precedent. Previously, military governments such as the one in Brazil had not given in to the demands of terrorist groups. Small guerrilla groups in Brazil and elsewhere realized that they had a powerful weapon in hostage-taking. The success of the young students lent encouragement to other revolutionary groups.

Indeed, within little more than a year, the Japanese, West German, and Swiss ambassadors to Brazil were all taken hostage by student groups and held for the ransoming of jailed prisoners. In each case, the government met the demands. One young terrorist, in an interview, explained: "In Brazil, the only way to get a person out of jail is through kidnapping. We have about 500 revolutionaries in jail. . . . We see nothing unfair in kidnapping an innocent person since the authorities arrest not only revolutionaries, but many ordinary people as well."[18]

CHAPTER FIVE

THE DISEASE SPREADS

It didn't take long for the "message" to spread. Soon, a group largely made up of university students in Uruguay picked up on the hostage-taking tactics that had been employed with such success in Brazil. This group, known as the National Liberation Movement, or more popularly the Tupamaros, spread terror through this tiny country for several years in a vain attempt to overthrow the democratic government.

But whereas kidnappings in Brazil turned out to be to the advantage of the revolutionaries, the kidnappings in Uruguay turned mostly sour for all involved. In July 1970, for example, the Tupamaros captured an American named Dan Mitrione, an Indiana police chief who had come to the South American country to assist the Uruguayan police. The kidnappers demanded, for his release, the freeing of several of their group members, who they said were being tortured in jail.

The similarities between the Brazilian and Uruguayan cases ended here. In the United States, President Richard M. Nixon stuck to a new hard line regarding hostage-taking. He declared that there would be no deals with rebels of any nation. Following this line, Uruguayan president Pacheco called the Tupamaros common thieves and said he would not release a single prisoner. This action sealed Mitrione's fate. He was executed by his captors.

The terrorist group later said that they felt they had to carry out this action to maintain the credibility of their kidnap-exchange policy. They had not believed President Pacheco when he had announced he would not free any of the jailed prisoners.

As the Tupamaros explained in an interview: "The kidnappings are part of an overall plan of harassment against the regime with the objective of obtaining the release of imprisoned comrades, and they are also—just like all the other attacks of our movement—aimed at undermining the foundations of the system, wearing it down, and overthrowing it."[19]

The killing of Mitrione proved to be the beginning of the end for the Tupamaros. For one thing, his death triggered a series of nasty reprisals by the Uruguayan government. A version of martial law was instituted. The government's general assembly voted to temporarily suspend private citizens' rights of property, assembly, personal liberty, and free expression.

The Uruguayan public, too, which had long been sympathetic to the students' cause, began to turn their backs. The murdering of an unarmed hostage, for whatever cause, was despised and looked upon as a cowardly act.

The Mitrione slaying and the kidnapping and killing of the West German ambassador to Guatemala during the same time period raised a serious moral question. Terrorists asked whether it was right for others to condemn them for using hostage-taking as a tactic to free

Dan Mitrione was taken hostage by Uruguayan terrorists in July 1970 and later killed.

comrades known to have been tortured in prison. Under these circumstances, they added, wouldn't any means be justified to achieve the ends?'

The majority of Uruguayans apparently felt that such killings could not be justified no matter what the cause, and public support deteriorated. Within two years, the parliament was dissolved in Uruguay and the military took over the government. They squashed the Tupamaros by jailing thousands of its members and supporters.[20]

Hostage-taking next surfaced in Argentina, with new twists. In Brazil, the act had worked for the terrorists. In Uruguay, it had backfired. But in Argentina, again, it became relatively successful.

The country was in a chaotic state in the early 1970s. Since the ouster of dictator Juan Peron in the mid-1950s, Argentina had been badly ruled by both civilian and military governments. Tens of thousands of Argentines had been unjustly imprisoned, tortured, or killed. Millions lived in squalor. Such conditions bred a number of terrorist groups who sought to aid the poor and overthrow the corrupt leaders. Some of these groups used the weapon of hostage-taking to achieve their goals, but instead of snatching the diplomats of foreign governments, they chose important businessmen.

One of the first victims was a British executive named Stanley Sylvester, who worked for Swift and Company, a large meat-packing firm. Sylvester was ransomed for $62,500, which the company quickly paid. This money was then used to buy food, clothing, and school supplies for the poor.

Next, a revolutionary group captured Oberdan Sallustro, president of the Italian Fiat automobile company in Argentina. The group first asked $800,000 for his release, to be paid in school supplies, and for the freeing of fifty political prisoners. But Argentine leaders tried to stop any deal, declaring that no bargains should be struck with terrorists. This led to the ransom being raised to more than $4 million. But before Fiat officials could meet with the kidnappers, police found the hideaway where Sallustro was being held. There was a fierce gun battle, and Sallustro was found dead in the assaulted house, his body riddled with bullets.

Although this hostage effort failed, terrorists nevertheless realized they could make a lot of money by kidnapping business people. Subsequently, a rash of such abductions took place. In one six-week period in 1973, guerrilla groups captured two English executives, a West German clothing manufacturer, the president of the Firestone Tire and Rubber Company in Argentina, the vice-president of an Italian bank, and a New York bank executive. These kidnappings alone brought in more than $8 million in ransom money.

By the end of the year, millions more dollars were paid to secure the release of business people employed by such companies as Coca-Cola, Ford, and Kodak. Terrorists reportedly collected more than $14 million from Exxon Corporation alone.

Such frenzied activity led to what amounted to a state of siege in the Argentine capital of Buenos Aires. Thousands of executives from the United States and other countries were recalled or transferred. Those who remained hired teams of bodyguards and lived in constant fear.

Much of the ransomed money was used to help overthrow the corrupt and inept government, and in late 1973 former dictator Juan Peron was brought back to rule once again. But he was now seventy-eight years old, and was no longer able to control things. A virtual civil war broke out in Argentina, and by the mid-1970s, with Peron dead and his second wife, Isabella, deposed as the country's leader, thousands of antigovernment guerrillas were killed or jailed, halting the taking of individual hostages for large fees.[21]

CHAPTER SIX

ASSAULT ON EUROPE

As the kidnapping terrorist groups faded from the scene in South America, under the harsh, repressive regimes of the military dictatorships of the late 1960s and early 1970s, a new wave of hostage-taking began surfacing halfway around the world, in Europe.

During the decade of the 1970s, terrorism was to take many forms in many countries. Terrorists hit targets in Great Britain, West Germany, Italy, Sweden, Holland, Belgium, France, Spain, Portugal, Austria, Switzerland, and Greece. The tactics used were brutal. Bombs were set off indiscriminately in crowded stores, shops, restaurants, and transportation centers, often killing dozens of people and injuring hundreds. Business leaders and government officials were shot or kidnapped. Terror spread across the continent.

One of the bloodiest organizations of the era was the notorious Baader-Meinhof gang, which wreaked havoc throughout West Germany in a futile attempt to topple the democratic government in power. Precisely what their own ideology was, was never made clear. They claimed to be Marxist communists, but even the East German Communist party renounced them and their methods, calling them "disappointed middle-class children without revolutionary discipline and without fundamental political knowledge."[22]

However, they did succeed not only in creating widespread fear but also in changing the lifestyle of many of West Germany's political and industrial leaders. For example, a chief executive officer of one of the world's largest chemical companies, headquartered in West Germany, told this author some of the measures he and many others were forced to take for their own protection. "I carry a pistol with me everywhere I go now," he said. "My chauffeur does, too. He doubles as my bodyguard." He added that he never took the same route from his home to his office, or back to his home more than once. This was to keep terrorists from tracking his movements. And he was always on the alert for anything unusual, such as a stalled car on the road, that might signal an intended ambush.

The Baader-Meinhof gang never really gained support from the general public, as the Tupamaros once had in Uruguay. When two leaders of the group were captured and imprisoned in the early 1970s, much of the gang's power was lost, although sporadic killings, bombings, and kidnappings continued for some time afterward.

Although the Baader-Meinhof gang's purposes were rather abstract and hazy, the terrorist activities of another group further north in Holland were clearly aimed at achieving a specific purpose. In December 1975, six men carrying machine guns, a pistol, and a hunting rifle boarded a four-car electric train in the Dutch town of Assen. Minutes later, they stopped the train, killed the locomotive's engineer, and held more than fifty passengers hostage.

As police and soldiers ringed the idle train, another

group of related terrorists struck in the capital city of Amsterdam, forcing their way into the Indonesian consulate and taking another forty-one prisoners, including sixteen children. For the next three days, as the entire world watched entranced via satellite television, an eerie stalemate grew between the gun-bearing revolutionaries and the authorities.

The terrorists were South Moluccans from Indonesia seeking independence for their homeland, a cluster of eight hundred Spice Islands in the Indonesian archipelago. Many Moluccans had fled from these islands when the Dutch colonial empire there collapsed in 1949 and an independent government in Jakarta took control. The natives had never forgiven the Dutch for this, and now they demanded that the Netherlands government intercede to help them gain independence for the islands.

Although the goal was specific, the chances of achieving it were nil, for the Dutch no longer had any influence in Indonesia. Still, the Moluccans wanted attention drawn to their plight, and in this effort, they succeeded.

At the end of three days, the six men holding the hostages on the train released them and surrendered. The Moluccans in the consulate gave up several days later, after the Dutch authorities assured them they were at least willing to talk about the situation.

But this case was another one in which hostage-taking eventually proved to be a disadvantage to the terrorists. Dutch opinion ran high against the Moluccans, and instead of gaining sympathy for their cause, they managed only to stir up anger. This anger reached even greater heights a year and a half later, when another faction of the group captured a schoolhouse in the village of Bovensmilde and held 105 school children and five teachers prisoner. After four tense days, however, when the children became ill with stomach viruses, the Moluccans released them, failing again in their bid to gain support to free the Moluccan Islands.[23]

Another famous case of hostage-taking in the 1970s that backfired occurred in Italy. There, the ruling government for more than thirty years after World War II had been generally bureaucratic and inefficient, causing broad unrest, especially among young people. The young militants had hoped to find their answers to a better Italy through the Communist party, but the Italian Communists, they eventually decided, compromised too much with government leaders in power.

And so a new terrorist organization known as the Red Brigades surfaced. Like the Baader-Meinhof gang in West Germany before them, they sought to bring down the incumbent administration through a war of terror. Bombings, assassinations, and kidnappings became almost regular events in Rome, Milan, and other large cities. The Red Brigades struck with swiftness, efficiency, and a brutality unmatched since the days of Hitler. Again, fear swept through the country, as the unprepared Italian police and military forces proved to be almost helpless.

Then, in March 1978, the rebels staged one of the most daring and dramatic hostage-grabbings in history. They ambushed the car of Italian prime minister Aldo Moro, killed five of his bodyguards, and abducted Moro. This shocked Italy and the rest of the world as no other kidnapping had since that of the Lindbergh baby in the 1930s.

The abduction of Moro made the Red Brigades seem invincible. For if they could capture a renowned leader such as Moro in broad daylight and get away with it, it proved that no one, in Italy or elsewhere, was invulnerable.

As the days of Moro's captivity stretched into weeks, the Italians launched one of the most massive manhunts in history in an effort to find their leader. Thousands of

*The kidnapping of Italian Prime Minister
Aldo Moro resulted in one of the
biggest manhunts in modern history.
Moro was later found slain.*

extra policemen were drafted from all over the country. Backed by new antiterrorist laws, quickly passed by the government, they conducted one of the most intensive and extensive searches. In Rome alone, 25,000 men scoured the city. Still, they found nothing.

The Red Brigades, meanwhile, made it known what they wanted in exchange for sparing the prime minister's life. They demanded the release of thirteen of their members then being held in jail, including one of their top leaders. But the Italian government took a strong, hard-line stand, saying they would release no one. Interestingly, Moro himself had long been a staunch advocate of such a policy. Although the Italian people wept and prayed for Moro's safe release, they supported their government's position.

Fifty-four days after he had been captured, Moro was found dead in the trunk of a car in Rome, his body riddled with bullets. Moro became a symbol. Many Italians who had felt some sympathy for the Brigades' cause now turned against it. In time, the revolutionary movement faltered, having lost what popular appeal it had. Many of its members were killed or caught and imprisoned.[24]

CHAPTER SEVEN

KIDNAPPING AT 30,000 FEET

One of the most dramatic forms of hostage-taking over the past quarter of a century has been skyjacking, or the hijacking of jet airplanes loaded with passengers. Terrorists have chosen to use this form for a variety of reasons. First, it attracts immediate and global media coverage. A skyjacking is front-page, prime-time news. Because the lives of so many people are endangered, anywhere from dozens to hundreds in some cases, the captors know their demands will be dealt with swiftly by government officials. Skyjackings cannot be ignored. Also, the terrorists can use the aircraft as their own escape vehicle to nations that may be sympathetic to their cause.

Yet, curiously, this "weapon" was not initially used much by terrorists. The first skyjackings in the late 1950s and early 1960s were usually carried out by half-crazed men and women who were merely seeking passage to generally forbidden destinations. In the United States, in particular, many planes were diverted from their normal flightpaths to carry skyjackers to Cuba. Once the skyjackers left the aircraft, usually in Havana, the plane and its passengers then were free to fly back to the United States.

At first, it was a relatively easy task to hijack a plane, even if a person was acting alone, which was often the case. Twenty-five years ago, airport security was extremely lax. There were no metal detectors in airport terminals to check if anyone boarding a plane was armed with a weapon. Consequently, hijackers could easily smuggle aboard guns, even rifles or submachine guns, knives, explosives, hand grenades, bombs, or just about anything else.

But, as the incidents of aircraft hijackings increased, the United States and other nations began taking security measures. One of the most effective, and one that has changed forever the appearance and atmosphere of airports, was the addition of metal-detection devices. Today, we take these for granted, hardly noticing them as we walk through a terminal en route to boarding a plane. Both passengers and the luggage they carry with them are checked, and whenever heavy metallic devices are detected by the sophisticated equipment, a familiar alarm is sounded. Usually, someone has too many keys, pens, or pocket change, and once this is determined, they are allowed to pass on through. Potential skyjackers know that there is now little chance in this country and in most other countries around the world of sneaking a weapon through such a system, and this has greatly helped reduce the number of attempted skyjackings.

Also effective have been the bilateral agreements concerning hijackers that have been worked out between the United States and Cuba. Cuba does not want hijacked planes entering its country. Most of the people who perpetrate such acts are unstable or revolutionary by nature, not the type of person that most nations would welcome. Consequently, Cuba instituted a policy of either jailing the hijackers on the spot and giving them harsh prison sentences or returning them immediately to the United States so they could be taken into custody for trial and sentencing there.

Similar measures were taken in many other countries. In fact, in the handling of skyjackers, most countries are in agreement. Perpetrators must be severely punished so as to discourage recurrences of the act. This came across clearly in three important international conventions: in Tokyo, Japan, in 1963; in the Hague, Netherlands, in 1970; and in Montreal, Canada, a year later.[25]

For a time, from the mid- to late 1970s, incidents of aircraft hijackings decreased sharply. But in the early 1980s, they began to rise again; only this time, most of the incidents were perpetrated by hard-core terrorist groups with their now-familiar demands. Generally, planes were seized and passengers were held hostage in an effort either to gain instant recognition for the captors' cause or in an effort to free comrades being held in prisons for past terrorist acts.

Some of these acts were successful because they were staged in airports around the world where proper security measures had not been taken. This was particularly true in some nations in the Middle East and in a few European countries, most notably Greece.

For a while in the mid-1980s, the frequency of such hijackings frightened travelers. There were many dramatic incidents in which planeloads of passengers were held captive for days or weeks at a time as negotiations between terrorists and government officials dragged on.

The skyjacking of TWA Flight 847 en route from Athens to Rome on June 14, 1985, with 153 persons aboard, was a good example of how small bands of revolutionaries could tie entire national governments up in knots—in this case, the United States. In fact, in this instance, the terrorists took great pleasure in showing the world how they could thumb their noses at the United States. Shortly after the plane was seized, the Lebanon-based group called the Islamic Jihad claimed responsibility for the deed and said they wanted to "prove to America that we can hit you anywhere we want."

The group threatened to kill the plane's crew and passengers unless seventeen Shiites imprisoned in Kuwait for bomb attacks were freed, as well as seven hundred other Shiite prisoners being held in Israel. The gun-brandishing terrorists had the airliner fly to Beirut, Lebanon. Over the next three days, most of the passengers were released, but forty of them were driven to secret hideouts within the battle-torn city.

For several days, the event captured world attention, and the radical Shiite captors knew how to keep the television cameras rolling. At one point, they even invited journalists out to the TWA plane, where they still held the flight crew captive. Pilot John Testrake warned the television audience that if any rescue attempt was made, "We'd all be dead men."

Later, five of the passenger-hostages were brought before TV cameras for a forced press conference where they, too, pleaded with the Reagan administration "to refrain from any form of military or violent means as an attempt . . . to secure our freedom." The hostages said this would "cause additional unneeded and unwarranted deaths among innocent people," and they urged that Israel resolve the crisis by releasing the Shiite prisoners.

Experts warned that if the terrorists' demands were not met, the hostages, hidden in several secluded areas throughout Beirut, might be held prisoner indefinitely. Said Brian Jenkins, a terrorism specialist for the Rand Corporation, "We're not talking about a hijacking anymore. This is a new kind of hostage situation that could last a long time—weeks and conceivably even months."

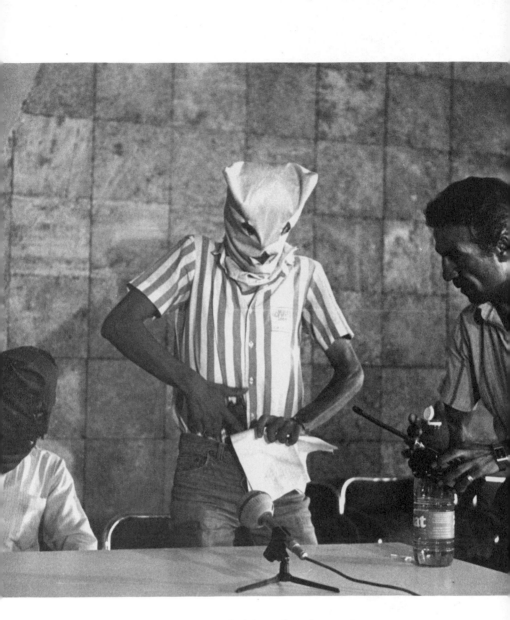

A *hooded hijacker from TWA Flight 847 places his gun in his pants before reading a statement to the press.*

The TWA hostages were released after three tense weeks when the United States and Israel agreed to develop a phased plan to free the seven hundred Shiite prisoners. But President Reagan and other world leaders were fearful that this was too steep a price to pay. They felt that the action could be seen as capitulation to terrorist demands, which could trigger yet more hostage seizures and other terrorist acts.[26]

Oddly, however, the number of airplane hijackings dropped sharply after this. For one thing, bowing to public pressure, countries where airport security was poor began to tighten up their security. Greece, for example, which had lost hundreds of millions of dollars in annual income when thousands of American and other tourists began canceling their trips there, made a number of improvements in airport security.

Another reason for the decline in skyjackings was that the terrorists realized the dangers to themselves when they used this particular form of hostage-taking. For example, if the aircraft crew refused to cooperate while in flight, the terrorists were immediately faced with the decision of whether to destroy the plane and crew—and themselves in the process.

Even if the crew cooperated and flew them to wherever they wanted to go, they eventually would have to land, and there they faced more problems. Squadrons of police or soldiers would surround the aircraft, which would either be out of fuel or could be disabled by shooting out its tires. The hostage-takers would then be sitting ducks. All they would have left is the threat of killing hostages. If they actually murdered passengers on board, the plane might then be stormed by armed soldiers and the hijackers could only surrender or be killed by superior forces. If they didn't kill any hostages, the authorities would wait it out until the terrorists gave up.

Finally, terrorists decided it was much safer for them, much simpler to plan, and much easier to carry out individual kidnappings of diplomats and others than it was to hijack an aircraft. Thus, by the mid- to late 1980s, there were fewer skyjackings and more kidnappings, especially in the Beirut area.

The era of aircraft hijacking may not be entirely over. But tighter security measures in most of the airports around the world have made seizing a plane a much riskier enterprise.

CHAPTER EIGHT

THE IRANIAN DEBACLE

One of the most famous incidents of hostage-taking of our time was the Iranian crisis, in which more than fifty Americans were held prisoner in Tehran and in other locations in Iran for 444 days, lasting from November 4, 1979, to January 20, 1981. More than any other single similar event in history, with the possible exception of the Lindbergh baby kidnapping in 1932, the Iranian situation captured, and maintained throughout its duration, the attention of not only the United States but of the entire world.

During this prolonged period, not a single day went by without some major news coverage of the hostages and their plight. Agonizingly slow and tedious negotiations for the Americans' release were followed to the tiniest detail, and a disastrous attempt to free the hostages by force made television network newscasts and front-page headlines for weeks.

Among other things, the Iranian case emphatically demonstrated how effective a weapon hostage-taking could be when used by terrorists or a second-rate power. And it again clearly showed how helpless it could render a major world power such as the United States. The U.S. administration, under President Jimmy Carter, tried every means it had to free the hostages, and nothing worked. Many political experts, in fact, believe it was Carter's failure to gain release for the captive Americans that led to his defeat in the 1980 presidential elections.

The hostilities leading up to the takeover of the U.S. embassy by Iranians on November 4, 1979, had been smoldering for years. There had been widespread unrest, punctuated by periodic rioting in the country during the last several months of the iron-fisted rule of the shah of Iran, Mohammed Reza Pahlavi.

On January 16, 1979, fearing for his life, the shah left Iran, paving the way later that month for the return of his bitterest political enemy, the Ayatollah Ruhollah Khomeini. Khomeini came out of exile in France to the cheers of millions of his countrymen, promising them he would transform Iran into an "Islamic republic."

Throughout this period of internal turmoil, there was deep-rooted resentment toward the United States because of its long-time support of the hated shah. There had even been a prophetic warning of things to come when, on February 14, 1979, a mob stormed the U.S. embassy in Tehran and took about a hundred Americans hostage. However, within hours, key Khomeini ministers had intervened and had persuaded the mob to release the hostages and leave the embassy.

Over the next few months, as the shah traveled around the world, anti-American resentment continued

There were numerous demonstrations against the Shah of Iran (above) and Americans during the so-called Iranian crisis of the late seventies and early eighties. The picture on the posters is of the Ayatollah Khomeini, who became the leader of Iran after the shah fled.

to build in Iran. It reached fever pitch in late October and early November 1979, when it was learned that the shah, now in ill health, had been secretly flown to New York for medical treatment.

The Iranian ire spewed over on November 4, when a throng of militant students broke down the gates surrounding the U.S. embassy and stormed the building Dozens of American workers in the embassy were captured, blindfolded, and their hands bound with plastic tape. Some were badly beaten by their captors, who screamed "Long live Khomeini!" Many of the new hostages were then taken outside to face tens of thousands of shouting Iranians.

This proved to be a horrifying experience. As one hostage recalls, "they were yelling, 'Death to the Americans' over and over until it was like an earthquake. It sounded like the walls were going to come down on top of me. The whole building was shaking. I have never been so terrified of anything in my whole life."

In the mass confusion that ensued during the first hours of the takeover, a number of Americans tried to escape. All but six were caught, but these six managed to hide out for several days and eventually made their way safely to the Canadian embassy. Some time later they were secreted out of the country to freedom.

In all, more than fifty Americans were held hostage by the Iranian students. The seizure caused outrage around the world, but the Khomeini government refused to do anything about the situation. Many experts felt it couldn't have freed the Americans if it had wanted to, because the students were acting on their own. President Carter quickly dispatched representatives to Iran to seek a negotiated settlement, but Khomeini announced he would not even see them.

For many of the hostages, the first few days and weeks in captivity were the worst. Most of them remained bound to chairs or handcuffed and blindfolded. They could not speak to each other, take showers, or even exercise. They were allowed to go to the bathroom only occasionally. The food was bad and not plentiful.

Periodically, during the first days, hostages were taken to separate rooms and interrogated. The Iranian students acted as if all the Americans were CIA spies. Some of the hostages were taken outside to face hostile crowds. Others were humiliated in front of television cameras. Some were beaten, often for little or no reason. In more than one instance, a hostage was made to suffer through a "game" of Russian roulette, where his captor would load a bullet into the chamber of a revolver, spin the chamber, place the gun to the hostage's head, and pull the trigger. Several times, others were threatened with death. They were taken out in the dead of night and made to believe they were going to be executed. The mental torture was terrible.

Treatment of individual prisoners varied greatly. Some were questioned only infrequently and then for only a few minutes at a time. Others were hauled before angry students almost daily and had to suffer through sessions that lasted hours, usually in uncomfortable surroundings.

Two weeks after the embassy takeover, the first break in the hostage stalemate occurred. Thirteen Americans—five women and eight black men—were released and sent home, leaving fifty-two others still in captivity.

The Ayatollah Khomeini later said he had ordered the release of the thirteen because Islam has a high regard for women and because blacks in the United States are oppressed. Inexplicably, two women and one black man were still held.

Shortly after this, several of the hostages were taken to a warehouse basement on the embassy grounds and held there. There were no windows, and one person described it as being similar to living in a tomb. He said that they couldn't see or hear anything. They were completely cut off from the outside world.

*An American hostage is led blindfolded by
Iranian students in front of a crowd shouting
"Death to Carter, Yankee Go Home!"*

The Iranians wanted the shah returned to their country so that he could be tried before his people. Only this, the captors said, could secure the release of the hostages. The United States, however, would not give in to that demand. Still, great efforts were being made on many fronts to reach a solution to the problem. On December 4, for example, the UN Security Council called for the Americans' release in a unanimous vote. But the Iranians ignored all this.

In an effort to further their cause, the Iranians interviewed some of the hostages on television. In these tapes, the Americans were critical of the U.S. policy protecting the shah. But the interviews did not accurately reflect the views of those who made the statements. They later said that they were forced to do it for propaganda purposes.

When word leaked out in January 1980 that six Americans had escaped with the help of Canadian embassy officials, the Iranian guards reacted angrily. In one heart-stopping incident, twenty-one of the remaining hostages were rounded up by seven guards wearing masks and wielding automatic rifles. The Americans were lined up against a wall, and the guards aimed their rifles at them, firing-squad style. Hostage Richard Queen recalled later, "I knew it was my last moment. I said the Lord's Prayer . . . because I was sure that we had just breathed our last."

But there was no shooting. The hostages were returned to their rooms, badly shaken from the experience but glad to be alive.

Throughout the 444-day ordeal, there were many peaks of hope and valleys of despair for the hostages. In April 1980, for instance, it appeared that the deadlock in the negotiations had been broken. Iranian leaders had tentatively agreed to the setting up of a UN commission that would serve as a forum for Iran's grievances against the shah. In return for this, the hostages would be released. But, at the last moment, the unpredictable Khomeini reneged on the agreement.

When this happened, President Carter cut off diplomatic relations with Iran and secretly gave the go-ahead for a military rescue mission to free the Americans. The plan called for a surprise commando raid on the embassy. First, several helicopters and C-130 transport planes would land in the Great Salt Desert, about 200 miles (320 km) from Tehran. From there, the helicopters would refuel and ferry troops to the mountains just outside the city. The commandos would then drive into Tehran in unmarked cars and trucks that had been supplied by intelligence agents who had secretly entered the country. Under air cover from military planes, the commandos would assault the embassy and free the hostages. They would return to the desert and be flown out of the country. It was to be a quick-hitting, forceful operation not unlike the one successfully pulled off by Israeli soldiers who freed hostages in 1976 at Entebbe, Uganda (see Chapter 11).

Many experts, including some of President Carter's closest advisers, were fearful of the mission. They were afraid that a number of the hostages, perhaps all of them, might be murdered by their captors before the rescue could be carried out. Even if it worked, they feared it might lead to a major military confrontation with Iran, which possibly could draw in the Soviet Union.

As it was, however, the rescue attempt never came off. Four of the helicopters broke down either en route to the desert location or on the ground. President Carter ordered the mission aborted, but as the commandos boarded their craft in the desert, one of the helicopters collided with a C-130 transport, and eight members of the military team were killed. It was the low point in the entire Iranian hostage drama. Worse, the captive Americans were then separated, and many were taken to hiding places in Tehran and other cities around the country to discourage further rescue attempts.

Following this drama, the hostages suffered a different kind of fate—crushing boredom, loneliness, and doubt. A few endured the agonies of months of solitary confinement in dark, windowless dungeons or closets. Conversation, fresh air, exercise, news, mail, and showers were forbidden. The days dragged on endlessly with little hope.[27]

Then, on July 27, 1980, the shah died. The demands of the captors, that the shah be returned to Iran, could never be met now. Some thought this would bring a quick end to the hostage situation. But it did not. The Iranians demanded that the United States acknowledge its past "imperialistic" role in Iran and return the shah's wealth to the country.

In November 1980, Ronald Reagan was elected president of the United States; it was hoped this would have a positive effect on the release of the hostages, but the negotiations continued to move slowly. Khomeini then began changing the conditions for a release. He now wanted the United States to "unfreeze" certain Iranian financial assets being held outside of the country. Some of these demands were complex and difficult to understand and therefore hard to fulfill.

But ever so slowly, progress began to be made. At last, on January 20, 1981, the last obstacles of the agreement were overcome, and the Americans were freed.

It had been a long, harrowing experience, not only for the hostages but for all Americans, including President Carter, who had felt helpless for such a long time. But whereas the United States had appeared to be humiliated and demoralized by a much weaker nation during this period, the release and return of the Americans seemed to solidify the nation. The hostages were treated as national heroes, and the United States, which had been torn apart internally only a few years before by the Vietnam War, seemed truly united once more in celebration.

CHAPTER NINE

THE LEBANESE CONNECTION

In the past few years, the number one site of most terrorist hostage-takings has shifted to the Middle East and Lebanon, specifically Beirut, Lebanon's capital. In this battle-scarred city, torn by warring factions throughout the 1980s, scores of diplomats, government officials, business executives, clergymen, media representatives, and others have literally been swept off the streets by fanatical splinter groups and taken prisoner. Their captors are cold, hard, and fearless, often abducting their targets in broad daylight. They ambush people in cars or strongarm them on foot, quickly whisking them away to prearranged secret hideaways.

There are few attempts at rescue or escape because the terrorists are heavily armed with automatic weapons and have not hesitated to brutally murder anyone who gets in their way. Some hostages, too, have been killed by these zealots, while others have been held for months, in some cases even years, as negotiations for their release have dragged on and on.

A war-torn street in Lebanon

Hope for release of hostages still in Beirut is often lost in a sea of complexity, because there are so many shadowy, little-understood political organizations involved who are often at odds even with each other. However, it is generally believed that most kidnappings have had the sanction of such terrorist-supporting countries as Iran, Libya, and Syria.

Extremist Shiite Moslems form the principal group responsible for airliner hijackings and individual kidnappings from the mid-1980s on. There are an estimated 90 million Shiites spread throughout the Middle East, representing about 10 percent of the world's 900 million Moslems. Only about one million Shiites are in Lebanon, but among them are many of the key leaders of terrorist attacks across the Middle East and Europe over the past few years.

One of the most fearsome groups of Shiites has been the Islamic Jihad, which has claimed responsibility for many bombings, shootings, and hostage-taking incidents in recent years. The Jihad was inspired by the Islamic revolution of the Ayatollah Khomeini in Iran, and like the ayatollah's millions of followers, they foster hatred of the United States. Thus, Americans in Beirut have been key targets for kidnappings.

Intelligence experts believe that the Islamic Jihad operates terrorist centers in Iraq, Kuwait, Bahrain, and Saudi Arabia, as well as in Lebanon. It is also strongly suspected that terrorists there receive organizational support and training from Khomeini's Iranian forces.[28]

It appears that the short-term goal of the Jihad is to force the release of Shiites being held in Kuwaiti and Israeli prisons. This has been their number one demand in exchange for the freedom of hostages they have held. Their ultimate ambition, however, is to form a new Islamic order throughout the Middle East and to punish the United States for its long-term support of Israel.

Shiite activists are convinced that their religious roots and Islamic traditions give them special strength, and they have an unwavering commitment to spread their brand of fanaticism throughout Lebanon and beyond. To achieve this goal they believe that the U.S. presence in the region must be completely eliminated.[29]

One of the most highly publicized hostage-taking incidents in Lebanon in recent years involved the American journalist Charles Glass. His case was strikingly similar in many respects to most of the kidnappings in and around Beirut in recent years, with one key exception—Glass escaped.

In June 1987, Glass, in Lebanon to gather material for a book, was driving through the battered slums on the outskirts of Beirut with two Lebanese friends when a Mercedes cut in front of their car. Suddenly, four or five men jumped out of the Mercedes, and several others, all armed, got out of a car behind the one Glass was in.

At gunpoint, they dragged Glass into the Mercedes and sped him to a hideaway within the city, in a building with an Iranian flag in front of it. Glass was the twenty-fourth foreigner to be listed as "missing, presumed kidnapped" in Lebanon. He soon learned that his captors were members of the Iranian-supported Shiites.

Like so many other hostages before him, Glass was blindfolded and chained to a bed for days. Over the next several weeks, he managed to drop notes asking for help, often written in his own blood, out the building's windows. But the Shiites found the notes and later moved him to another building, a common tactic used by terrorists in Lebanon today.

After two months in captivity, Glass was somehow able to escape. He got a ride to Damascus, Syria, and later flew home to the United States.[30]

Another celebrated Lebanese case, which began two years earlier, also ended in a hostage's freedom, but this time it involved the mechanism of international politics, both overtly and covertly, rather than a dash to freedom. In this incident, David Jacobsen, at the time director of Beirut's American University Hospital, was accosted and kidnapped on a Beirut street by six members of the Islamic Jihad on May 28, 1985.

The U.S. government dealt behind the scenes for months to secure his release. Jacobsen became involved in what would later become known as the Iran-Contra affair (see Chapter 15). Briefly, Reagan administration officials negotiated secretly with Iranian officials to sell military arms to them for monies that would ultimately be used to provide weapons (without congressional approval) to pro-U.S. forces in Nicaragua. As an incentive to this dealing, Iran said it would intervene on behalf of the United States in an attempt to free American hostages, including Jacobsen, being held in Lebanon. In addition to selling the arms to Iran, the United States agreed to pay a ransom for each released hostage, reportedly from $1 million to $3 million per person.

When the press broke the story of the secret deal after Jacobsen's release, there was a great public clamoring against the lapse in official U.S. policy not to give money—or arms—to terrorists. At this point, the hostage-release program fell apart, and no additional hostages were freed.

It was during this same period of time that another event, not related to the Iranian arms-sale deal, came to light, and it, too, had a direct bearing on Jacobsen's fate. This event involved Syria, which exerts considerable influence on Lebanese terrorist groups.

What happened was that Western intelligence sources tied Syria to a planned bombing of an El Al airliner. Though the bombing never came off, it was revealed that the terrorists involved had received assistance from the Syrian embassy in London.

When this came to light, Great Britain broke off diplomatic relations with the government in Damascus, and the United States followed suit by withdrawing its ambassador from Syria. "When a country does that [supports terrorism], it isolates itself from the civilized world," said Secretary of State George Shultz.

Embarrassed by this public disclosure, Syrian president Hafez Assad used his influence, with strong U.S. government urging, to help free Jacobsen. In November 1986, seventeen months after his capture, Jacobsen got in one of three cars that had pulled up in front of the old U.S. embassy building in Beirut. This convoy, escorted by two truckloads of Lebanese police, then drove Jacobsen out of the city, where he was released.

Such behind-the-scenes wheeling and dealing goes on continuously. Sometimes it is successful, and sometimes it isn't. Jacobsen was lucky. Had not Syria been exposed as a terrorist-supporting state, Assad might not have become involved, and Jacobsen might still be in captivity somewhere in Beirut.[31]

As this book went to press, nine Americans were still being held hostage in Lebanon. Among them were Joseph Cicippio, American University comptroller; Frank Reed, director of a private elementary school in Beirut; Edward Tracy, a writer; Terry Anderson, a newspaperman; Beirut University College teachers Alan Steen, Jesse Turner, and Robert Polhill, who were abducted January 24, 1987; and U.S. Marine Lieutenant Colonel William Higgins, kidnapped in February 1988.

The U.S. government has assured the families of the hostages that all avenues available, both officially and unofficially, are being explored in efforts to free the nine Americans. But how long this will take is anyone's guess.

Beirut remains a smoldering hotbed for terrorism and hostage taking. However, due to precautions taken by the United States and other nations, future kidnappings should be held to a minimum. Most Americans, for instance, were long ago ordered out of Lebanon by the U.S. State Department and have left the country.

Experts believe that the remaining American hostages will eventually be set free. They cite as one reason for this the fact that U.S. hostages no longer command worldwide attention. They have become "old news."

Without the glare of international television and newspapers, the hostages' value to their captors has diminished. Terrorists, therefore, are more likely now to trade their prisoners for the best financial deal they can make with private individuals and corporations.

Above: recently freed hostage
David Jacobsen hugs his daughter
Diane on a flag-draped balcony
while her husband looks on.
Below: portraits of a number of
the hostages, most still being held,
in Lebanon

CHAPTER TEN

THE EMOTIONS
OF THE VICTIMS

What is it like to be the victim of a hostage-taking incident? The effect on a person is immediate, and often long-term. In some instances, hostages never fully recover from their kidnappings. Others dismiss it as soon as they are freed and go on with their lives. The range of physical and psychological effects varies greatly with the individual.

The emotions of a hostage range from initial shock and terror to long-term fear, worry, and anger. Some develop a bitterness toward life that is never overcome. Others will carry their fear forever, being afraid of participating in even the most commonplace events of everyday life that most of us take for granted.

Most of the victims who are held for long periods of time suffer from crushing boredom and deep depression. Almost always they are kept in the dark, not knowing what, if anything, is being done about their situation. Frequently they are kept bound and blindfolded. They are cut off completely from any communication with the outside world. They lose track of time and place. They become disoriented.

Many hostages live in constant fear of being killed at any moment. They view their captors as crazed madmen who have little respect for the value of human life. Even the smallest incident can set off a tantrum in a terrorist that may result in a beating or possibly a death.

Most of all, the victims are alone in hostile surroundings. They have little or nothing in common with their "guards," and they seldom know why they were taken prisoner in the first place. Even if they were taken as part of a group, they are rarely allowed to see or talk with other hostages, especially during the first few days or weeks of the kidnapping. It is, even under the best of circumstances, a miserable existence with which few, if any, of the hostages are prepared to cope.

How hostages are treated depends largely upon the whims of the group that kidnaps them. There seems to be no set pattern as to how the groups care for those they capture. Some are polite and respectful and try to make the victims as comfortable as possible. Others indiscriminately may beat or harass hostages, even against the orders of their superiors. Or, they may treat some of the hostages well and single out others for harsh punishment.

There have been instances of torture and some gruesome maimings, however. In a few highly publicized incidents, to prove that the person being held was still alive, one of his or her fingers or ears has been brutally cut off and sent to ransom payers. This, of course, is a grim tactic used to let it be known that the hostage takers will stop at nothing, including disfigurement and murder, to achieve their purpose. And, all too often, it works.

The torment and anguish of a hostage-taking can

also be damaging mentally and psychologically. In many cases, the victims are made to believe they are going to be brutalized or killed. And this fear can linger with them for years afterward. Many hostages have reported nightmares long after they have been released.

If there is a pattern to the treatment of those taken against their will, it usually follows something like this: The victim is seized by force. If the person resists, he or she is clubbed or beaten until submitting. Almost always, to protect the identity of the captors, the person is blindfolded and bound and then taken to a hideaway and generally placed in a room, cell, or basement. There may be a bed or cot and few other pieces of furniture. If there are windows, they are sealed shut and there is usually little light. If there is no toilet nearby, a bucket is left. Food is served infrequently and is usually not very nourishing.

As the kidnapping drags on, conditions may be relaxed in the weeks and months that follow. In time, the prisoners may be allowed to read books or write letters, and in some cases, they can watch television. They may also be allowed to talk with fellow prisoners or with their captors. And they are usually allowed to shower occasionally and exercise once in a while. But especially in long-duration cases, the life is boring and depressing. And the hostage never knows when some outside event may "change the rules" and make his or her life more miserable.

Although this is a "norm," if there is such a thing in hostage-taking, it by no means covers the full range of terrorist behavior. At times, hostages have been subjected to treatment that pushed them to the very limits of their endurance.

There have been instances, for example, where people have literally been buried alive—placed in coffin-like boxes, set in a hole in the ground, and been covered over with dirt, with only tiny air passages for breathing.

With no food or water, they have lived for several days under such conditions.

In 1971, Geoffrey Jackson, then the British ambassador to Uruguay, was captured by the Tupamaros, knocked out, bound with heavy steel wire, and put in a cage 3 feet (0.9 m) wide and 6 feet (1.8 m) long. He spent the better part of the next several months in that tiny cage. Others have been placed in solitary confinement for weeks or months at a time, with no human contact.

One Italian woman, kidnapped by the Red Brigades, spent thirty-five days manacled by the ankle to a bed in a small, damp room. There was no heat and no light. She could hardly move and was so cold she could not sleep many nights. Her captors packed her ears with wax and covered them with a sticky plaster to prevent her from hearing even the faintest of noises.[32]

Psychiatrists call such inhumane treatment "sensory deprivation," saying that when the mind is deprived of normal sensations such as sight and sound, and there is no human contact, it often hallucinates.

Geoffrey Jackson said that daydreaming helped him live through his 244-day ordeal. Experts say that the idea here is to transport the mind and spirit outside the prison walls to "rejoin society." American hostage David Jacobsen, who was held in a tiny room in Beirut, Lebanon, for seventeen months and finally released early in 1987, tells how he passed the time.

"To help myself through the hours, I spun an elaborate fantasy. I pretended I was with my family, getting ready to go to my son's wedding. In my mind, I went to the church and saw my future daughter-in-law coming in. I spent the whole day lost in my fantasy of what was happening thousands of miles away. I did the same thing on my son's birthday, and on my dad's birthday. I mentally drove up to see him and spent some time. Always, I tried to think of the good things in my life, the people I loved."[33]

Sometimes, the intense boredom is shattered by new waves of fear. Rocky Sickmann, a Marine guard at the U.S. embassy in Iran, spent 444 days as a hostage from 1979 to 1981. After three months, he and the other Americans being held had settled into somewhat of a routine existence. But one morning this changed abruptly. As he tells it:

"What a shock we had this morning around 3 A.M. All of a sudden the door opened and some [Iranian] students, masked and armed, came charging in, masking us, then taking us down the hallway. The first thing that popped into my mind was U.S. troops coming to try to evacuate us out, and the students knew it, so they were getting ready to waste us all. The students had told us if there ever was such an attempt to free us, we would all be shot.

"They [the students] faced us against the wall in the hallway. My whole body started to shake when I recognized the sound of bolts being forced home on a couple of rifles. I started to say my rosary when I was grabbed by the arm and taken into a room where I was told to face the wall and strip. I thought I was a goner for sure, and my body started to shake even more. I started to remember all the movies the students showed us earlier of all those dead people that were naked, lying in puddles of blood. I then started to think of myself just like one of them."[34]

As it turned out, this was only a scare tactic used by the Iranians as they searched the Americans' rooms. But it vividly shows the horrible mental torture victims can be exposed to at any time during their incarceration.

Paranoia can build up. A noise outside the room or cell may signal a guard coming to kill or beat a hostage. A police siren in the distance might mean the hideaway has been discovered and there will be a bloody shootout. Threats of imminent execution or mutilation have kept some hostages in a state of almost perpetual panic.

Perhaps even more terrifying than being suddenly hauled out in front of a potential firing squad in the middle of the night is being told when you are going to be killed. At least in Sickmann's case, he had no forewarning of what was going to happen, so he had no cause to fret or worry about it. But from a psychological standpoint, if you are told you are going to be killed on a certain date if ransom conditions are not met, the tension and anxiety build as that date nears.

Such was the case early in 1987 involving thirty-five-year-old French television engineer Jean-Louis Normandin, who was captured by pro-Iranian Moslem terrorists in Beirut, Lebanon. In return for Normandin, the kidnappers demanded the release of a convicted terrorist being held in jail in Paris.

When French president François Mitterrand rejected the proposed swap, the Moslems announced they would execute their hostage within forty-eight hours. When that deadline passed, others were set. Eventually, the captors were persuaded by Shiite Moslem religious leaders to cancel the execution.[35] Still, the psychological torture inflicted upon Normandin was almost unbearable.

Psychiatrists say that after the initial fear of death and torture passes, hostages often develop a feeling that they have been betrayed by their comrades or countrymen. Usually alone, cut off from other human company, without light or sound, the minds of hostages drift into a fog of paranoia, and with this comes a conviction, growing with each passing day, that they have been forgotten.

Many think of escape, but there is little hope of it. Very few political hostages have gotten away from their captors. The odds against them are too great. Most often, they don't know where they are. They may not speak the language. And generally, there are armed guards keeping watch on them.

British diplomat Jasper Cross, once held in Canada by a group known as the Quebec Liberation Front, said he thought about escape every day. "But every time I came up with the feeling that too much was against me. I never knew what was outside of the room in which I was held. I had no idea whether to turn left or right when I went outside, and every day I decided to hang on and that the chances were much better in staying alive for another 24 hours."[36]

In some cases, the captors try to indoctrinate the hostages with their political philosophies. In one of the most highly publicized hostage-taking cases of all time, a terrorist group called the Symbionese Liberation Army snatched newspaper publishing heiress Patty Hearst in California in 1974. She was just nineteen years old at the time.

In a tiny one-room apartment, she heard the group discuss their beliefs for weeks and became fascinated. In time, she actually joined the cause and took part in several of their raids, including bank robberies. Eventually, the leaders were killed in a fiery shootout with police, and Patty Hearst was captured, convicted of her crimes, and sent to prison.

In many other instances, hostages are forced to espouse the messages of the terrorist group that is holding them. Some are made to read statements denouncing their country's government and its leaders. Americans held in Iran and Lebanon have been made to do this on audio tapes or in front of television cameras.

And if they do not do as they are told—or if the terrorists suspect a trick—the consequences can be frightening. When American hostage David Jacobsen was told to write a letter critical of the U.S. administration, he did it. But his Lebanese captors believed that he was trying to somehow send hidden messages in the letter and accused him of being a spy. They took him into a room and beat his feet with a rubber hose.[37]

*Patty Hearst, heiress turned bank
robber, after being kidnapped by the terrorist
group the Symbionese Liberation Army*

Some hostages are forced to make "confessions" that they have spied for their country. They are ordered to appear on TV or make tapes to spread the word about the terrorists' cause, or to appeal for their government to make whatever deal the terrorists are demanding. Most hostages, once freed, disclaim any statements they made while in captivity, saying that they were made under the threat of beatings or death.

There is sometimes a strange phenomenon that takes place during kidnapping situations. It involves the developing relationships between the hostage-taker and the hostages. Part of the reason for the rough treatment, the blindfolds, and the harsh rules for no talking set down by captors has to do with the fact that they don't want to get to know their prisoners in the event they have to kill them. It is apparently much easier to kill a stranger than it is to slay someone you have grown to know and possibly like.

Yet the longer hostages are held, the more relaxed the rules become and the more familiar the two parties become. Psychiatrists contend that hostage-takers and hostages both are in such a highly charged mental state, each fearing death, that they become susceptible to emotional involvement with each other.

The hostage's fears are obvious. He or she could be killed at any moment. But the hostage-takers also realize that, from the moment they began the kidnapping, they put their lives on the line. They could be slain in a police shootout or, if captured, face either death or long prison sentences.

Against this background, peculiarly, hostages and their captors, at times, have formed very close and caring relationships with each other. This has come to be known as the "Stockholm Syndrome."

The name stems from an incident that occurred in Stockholm, Sweden, in August 1973. An escaped Swedish convict named Jan-Erik Olsson walked into one of the city's largest banks, pulled a submachine gun from under his jacket, and grabbed several hostages.

Swedish police sealed off the area, trapping Olsson and his prisoners inside, and thus began a tense stalemate that lasted for six days. During that time the hostages came to know Olsson, and he in turn developed feelings for them. On one occasion he put his coat around a female bank employee who was cold.

One evening in the bank, he asked another female employee if he might caress her, and she allowed him to do this. All during this time, the Swedish officials had taken a hard-line stance and refused to give in to Olsson's demands that he be allowed to escape, taking the hostages with him. As the days passed, the bank employees began to sympathize with their captor and actually tried to persuade the police to let him escape.

Eventually, the police threw tear gas into the bank's vault, and Olsson surrendered. But even after his capture, the hostages expressed tender feelings toward him. Later, police told Olsson that had he killed one hostage, they would have let him take the others and flee. He told them he had suspected that, but because of the kinship he had developed with them over the six days, he couldn't have brought himself to kill one.

In this particular case, as in many other hostage incidents, the victims initially think only of escape or survival, but after days or weeks of close contact with their captors, their feelings can turn to fondness and understanding. Psychiatrists contend that this is actually a return to infancy, when a baby depends upon everything from others. Thus, when hostages find themselves totally dependent upon other persons for survival, they revert to rather infantile behavior. They come to identify with their captors and often even sympathize with them. Conversely, they develop a certain degree of hostility toward the authorities who are trying to gain their release.[38]

For many hostages, the ordeal doesn't necessarily end with their release and return to freedom. Many have lingering psychological effects long afterward or have pronounced difficulty in readjusting to normal life.

The effects can include insomnia, nightmares, alcoholism, divorce, nervous breakdowns, and even suicide. Curiously, the length of time spent as a hostage seems to have little bearing on how quickly one readjusts. The aftershock can affect those held for only a brief time as well as those held for months or years. It depends on the individual.

The American Psychiatric Association's Task Force on Terrorism and its Victims has reported that ex-hostages experience a range of feelings, from guilt and fear to rage and helplessness. Two of the most common reactions, especially soon after release, are nightmares and insomnia, but these usually fade away in time.[39]

In recent years, better understanding of the post-hostage trauma has led to more effective treatment and increased the chances of total recovery. "These people are not mental cases," says Charles Figley, director of the Traumatic Stress Research Program at Purdue University in Indiana. "They are normal people reacting to an abnormal situation." Today, most mental-health officials recommend a "decompression period" for hostages immediately after release, to give them and their families time to digest their experiences and to prepare for the transition to life at home.[40]

But the kidnap victims themselves are not the only ones to suffer. Their families and friends do, too. Their feelings also span a wide range and include helplessness, guilt, rage, hope, depression, and despair.

Expressing her frustration, Mary Beth Streidel of Illinois, whose parents had been taken hostage aboard a jetliner in Lebanon, said, "Sit and wait—that's all you can do. And pray. It's the worst feeling in the world."

For most families there is a terrible sense of frustration in the uncertainty of the situation. The longer their friends and relatives are held, the greater the strain placed on them. For many, this sense of futility turns into rage, usually aimed at the home government and its leaders for failing to meet hostage-taker demands.

When the Reagan administration worked feverishly to free journalist Nicholas Daniloff, who was being held prisoner in Moscow in 1986, families of hostages in Lebanon became incensed. Said Margaret Say, whose brother was being held in Beirut: "There is a tremendous feeling of betrayal and outrage over President Reagan's refusal to negotiate with the Islamic radicals holding the Americans."[41]

Some family members have even defied government orders and flown to the hostage site to try to personally negotiate the release of their loved ones. Few are successful. For most families, like the hostages, it is a long, painful waiting game.

CHAPTER ELEVEN

SUCCESS AND DISASTER
IN RESOLVING
HOSTAGE CONFLICTS

Many experts believe strongly that the best and certainly the quickest means to bring a hostage situation to a solution is through the use of force—that is, to employ arms and manpower of significant strength and size to overpower hostage-takers. The element of surprise is often a key factor in such strategies. If the "enemy" can be taken off guard, the chances of success are much greater. But an enemy who realizes that his or her position is to be stormed in time might kill most or all of the hostages.

Like other methods for dealing with those holding hostages, force can sometimes be used with spectacular success. Or, such a tactic can end in cataclysmic failure. Following are two real-life cases in which force was used. One was hailed as a great victory against terrorism. The other resulted in death and disaster.

Eight minutes after an Air France Airbus carrying 242 passengers lifted off the runway at the airport in Athens, Greece, on June 27, 1976, a man and a woman stood up from their seats in the first-class section, each brandishing a pistol in one hand and a hand grenade in the other. As screams pierced the air, the woman aimed her gun at frightened stewardesses, while the man pushed his way into the cockpit. Over the plane's intercom system, he shouted, "My name is Basil Al Qubasi. The Popular Front for the Liberation of Palestine is in complete control of this flight. If you stay still and do nothing suspicious, no one will be hurt."

Thus began a harrowing experience that would last over the next several days. As one passenger later described it, "the atmosphere was very, very tense."

The skyjackers ordered the captain to divert the flight to Benghazi, Libya, a country that has been especially friendly to terrorists in recent years. There, a pregnant woman passenger was removed from the plane. Then the armed man and woman began collecting passenger passports, which they placed in a plastic bag. They pushed boxes near the doors, announcing that they contained explosives.

After six hours on the ground, the plane took off again, and six and a half hours later, it landed at Entebbe, Uganda, in the heart of Africa. There, the skyjackers made their demands known. They wanted Israel and four other nations to release fifty-three Palestinian terrorists being held in jail. If the conditions were not met, the hostages would be killed. The man and woman then herded the 242 passengers, plus the plane's crew members, into a cramped terminal building at the airport. Several other armed men on the ground joined the skyjackers in keeping close guard on the hostages.

Even as this was happening, Israeli officials in Tel Aviv quickly gathered to assess the situation and decide what to do. Israeli transportation minister Gad Yaakobi voiced what many were thinking: "If we give in to the hijackers' demands, the Palestinians will escalate their terror and no Israeli leaving the country will be safe."

Prime Minister Yitzhak Rabin asked his military

chiefs if there was a "military option" to be considered in rescuing the hostages. He was told that there was none at that time, because there was not enough information available. They needed more intelligence about the layout of the airfield, the number of hostages, and the risks involved should it be decided to attack the terrorists' position.

Rabin and his cabinet decided to explore the possibility of negotiating, but at the same time they ordered the military to draft a possible plan of attack. Over the next three days, a strike force was assembled and went into intensive training at a desert base in Israel. Meanwhile, intelligence officers began assembling data on every aspect of Entebbe. They checked flight routes into and out of Uganda and quizzed pilots who flew there.

Three days after the plane had been overtaken, the terrorists released all the non-Israeli passengers, reducing the number of hostages to 106. In Paris, the released passengers gave out vital information about the transit lounge in the terminal building. They said that there were no explosives wired to the building and that security was lax.

Negotiations continued, as the Israelis successfully stalled on the skyjackers' demands. During this time, more critical intelligence information was gathered. The U.S. Defense Department supplied satellite photos of Entebbe Airport, and Israeli agents were able to secretly get into the area and report back on the exact situation there. The neighboring country of Kenya told Israel that it could land a strike force there for refueling and that it would care for the wounded on the return flight.

On July 3, six days after the plane had been skyjacked, the Israeli cabinet met again to decide whether or not to send in the strike force. The vote was a unanimous yes.

Six huge aircraft were already standing by ready to

take off, including four Hercules C-130 cargo planes and two Boeing 707 jetliners. One of the jetliners was a command-and-communications center, the other a hospital plane. Escorted by Israeli Phantom jets, they flew south and over the Red Sea, Ethiopia, and Kenya. The hospital plane landed at Nairobi, Kenya, while the other aircraft continued on. The four Hercules planes skimmed over the shores of Lake Victoria and, in the dark of night, landed in the outlying reaches of Entebbe Airport.

As a diversion, the Israelis rolled a large Mercedes-Benz limousine out of one of the aircraft, along with two land rovers filled with ten Israeli commandos dressed in Palestinian uniforms. The limousine had license plates identical to those used by Uganda's notorious president, Idi Amin. As the car drove up to the terminal building, Ugandan soldiers snapped to attention. Under the cover of this diversion, the main commando force was able to rush up to within a few yards of the building without being detected.

Suddenly, shots rang out. The front windows of the building were shattered, and smoke and dust filled the lounges where the hostages were. They panicked, fearing they were about to be killed. The man who skyjacked the plane nearly a week earlier, later identified as German terrorist Wilfried Bose, raced into the lounge and aimed his submachine gun at the hostages, who were lying on the floor.

Many of the passengers thought he was about to shoot them. Curiously, however, he turned to the window and then was shot down himself. A short time later, the hostages heard the words *"Anachnu Israelim"* [We are Israelis], and then the first commandos entered the room. The shooting stopped outside, and the passengers ran toward the waiting transports.

Within twenty minutes, the hostages were in the air, heading toward Nairobi. Miraculously, all but three hostages made it. They had been killed in the crossfire;

also killed were the two terrorist skyjackers, twenty Ugandan soldiers, and one Israeli commando.[42]

To some, even this was too high a price to pay. But for the most part, the daring raid drew praise and admiration from around the world, especially from government leaders who had long been frustrated in their attempts to deal effectively with hostage-takers.

Said Israeli Prime Minister Rabin: "The basic principle is to fight the terrorists whenever you have a reasonable chance. You fight them in Jerusalem or you fight them in Entebbe, but you fight. You don't give in."[43]

In this case, the strategy and the gamble worked. But, as you will soon see, such tactics can also backfire.

The incident in question occurred in September 1972 at the twentieth Olympic Games, being held in Munich, West Germany. There, thousands of world-class athletes from all over the earth, countries large and small, were housed in an Olympic village. At 4:20 in the predawn blackness one morning, two telephone linemen saw a group of eight young men, carrying what was thought to be athletic gear, scale the 6-foot (1.8-m)-high fence that surrounded the village. The linemen thought only that they were athletes out for a night on the town and were sneaking back into their quarters.

However, the eight men were, in fact, Arab terrorists, members of a notorious group called "Black September." Once over the fence, they blackened their faces, donned hoods, and pulled automatic weapons out of their bags. They then stole their way through the quiet streets until they reached their destination—the housing quarters of the Israeli national Olympic team.

They banged on the door and asked, "Is this the Israeli team?" Wrestling coach Moshe Weinberg opened the door only a crack, and when he saw the hooded, armed terrorists, he yelled for the others in the apartment to escape. A burst of submachine-gun fire through the door felled Weinberg, and in seconds the terrorists were racing through the rooms. In a second apartment, an Israeli wrestler, trying to fend off the attackers with a knife, was shot to death.

Startled by the shouts and the gunshots, athletes ran to exit windows, and in the confusion, eighteen Israelis managed to escape. Nine others were taken hostage by the Arabs. They were bound hand and foot and shoved onto beds.

By 6 A.M., Munich police, alerted to the crisis by the athletes who had escaped, walled off the area surrounding the Israeli complex with a force of six hundred men. Police Chief Manfred Schreiber daringly walked up to the main apartment house and was met by the leader of the terrorists. Schreiber said later that he had thought of taking the Arab hostage himself, but the man apparently had considered that because he said, "Do you want to take me?" As he did, he opened up his hand. In it was a grenade.

By 9 A.M., the terrorists had made known their demands. They wanted two hundred Arab prisoners to be released from jails in Israel. They also wanted three other well-known terrorists freed—Ulrike Meinhof and Andreas Baader, leaders of a vicious band of German terrorists, and Kozo Okamoto, a Japanese revolutionary who had taken part in the massacre of twenty-six people at Tel Aviv's Lod Airport earlier in the year.

The eight Arabs, later identified as Palestinians, insisted that they and their prisoners be flown out of West Germany to any Arab nation except Lebanon or Jordan. They gave the authorities three hours to comply. If their demands were not met, they said, they would kill the hostages at the rate of two every half-hour.

In Israel, an emergency session of the government's cabinet was held, and a decision was quickly reached. They told German authorities they would not negotiate with the terrorists, nor would they release any prisoners.

An Arab terrorist looks out from the apartment where Israeli Olympic athletes were being held hostage.

They also said they would not object if the Germans allowed the terrorists to leave the country, provided that the hostages would first be freed.

Meanwhile, German authorities tried to negotiate. Interior Minister Hans-Dietrich Genscher personally took charge of the talks and offered the Palestinians an "unlimited" sum of money to release the hostages. He was turned down. Next, he offered himself and other officials as replacements for the Israelis, but he was rebuffed in that offer, also. He stalled by saying that he was having some success persuading Israel to reconsider releasing the jailed prisoners. This led to getting the deadline to kill hostages pushed back several times over the next twelve hours.

All the while these talks were taking place, German officials were mapping plans to attack the terrorists. Fifteen police sharpshooters, wearing armored vests, were assembled and brought to the scene. But it was decided not to let them fire on the Arabs who exposed themselves at apartment windows because there were too many others left inside who might slaughter the hostages if one or more of their own men were shot.

The drama dragged on, and by midafternoon, half the world was watching as television cameras panned the apartment area. At 3:45 P.M., at the request of the Israeli Parliament, the Olympic Games were suspended. All day long, sirens screamed and crowds gathered near the scene, creating an eerie, circus-like atmosphere.

West German Chancellor Willy Brandt flew to Munich from Bonn to personally supervise his government's operation. He immediately ruled out any possibility of allowing the terrorists to fly out of the country with the hostages. "That would be impossible for an honorable country to allow to happen," he said. "We are responsible for the fate of these people." Brandt called all the Arab leaders he could reach, pleading for them to intervene with the Palestinians, but he received no support from them.

With the terrorists by now getting edgy, the German authorities decided they would agree to a plan whereby the Arabs and their hostages would be taken to Munich's airport, put on a Lufthansa 727 jetliner, and flown to Cairo, Egypt. The Germans had no intention of carrying out this plan. They really hoped to ambush the terrorists at the airport. They felt that if they could kill the leader and a few others, the rest of the Palestinians might surrender. They began surrounding the airport with five hundred soldiers, including the sharpshooters.

It was 10 P.M. before the Arabs left the apartment complex, herding the prisoners, who were now blindfolded and tied together, onto a German army bus. It took them only a short distance to two awaiting helicopters, which airlifted them to the airport.

When they landed, the Arabs were cautious, never exposing more than four of their members at one time. The German sharpshooters had orders to fire whenever they saw the greatest number of terrorists in their sights. They fired, immediately killing two Arabs and wounding a helicopter crewman.

But they missed hitting the leader, who dived under a helicopter and fired back, knocking out the airfield lights as well as the radio in the communications tower. A Munich police sergeant was also killed.

For the next hour, the firing continued sporadically. Finally, after five of the terrorists had been killed, the other three surrendered. But all nine hostages had been murdered by the Arabs. Four had been machine-gunned and five others had burned to death when an Arab threw a grenade into the helicopter in which they were being held.[44]

So, in this case, the attempt to use force to free hostages failed completely. German authorities were heavily criticized for what many felt was a bungled attack. Critics said that negotiations should have been carried on further, and that the sharpshooters should not have fired the first shots unless there was a good chance that they could get all of the terrorists.

It was also argued that Germany was weak in its negotiating position because it had given into demands of terrorists on previous occasions. Most notable was a $5 million cash ransom to Palestinian skyjackers who had taken over a Lufthansa 747 jetliner in February 1972 with 186 passengers and crew members aboard.

Whatever, the sad fate of the Israeli Olympic hostages remains a grim reminder of what can happen when a rescue attempt goes awry.

CHAPTER TWELVE

THE ART OF
NEGOTIATING

The governments of some countries, such as Israel, stand firm and publicly declare they will not meet any terrorist demands. The set Israeli policy is, no deals of any kind, backed by the strong belief that any concessions only serve to encourage hostage-takers. But in the past fifteen years or so, more and more authorities worldwide have concluded that the best policy concerning the release of hostages may lie somewhere in between a hard-line stand of no concessions and one of total compliance to terrorist demands. This middle ground can be reached through the art of negotiating and often involves taking the hostage-takers down from their original, and usually impractical, goals to a more reasonable point where a deal can be made.

The tactic of negotiating began gaining strong support among government authorities and others after the Munich massacre of the eleven Israeli Olympic athletes in 1972. Experts began looking for a better way to deal with such volatile situations.

The policy of negotiating for hostage release began

in the United States. Two men are generally given credit for it: Simon Eisendorfer, a New York City police inspector, and Dr. Harvey Schlossberg, a New York City police detective with a doctoral degree in clinical psychology.

In 1972, Eisendorfer began studying cases involving hostages. This led him to the realization that incidents of hostage-taking were clearly on the rise, due partly to improvements in communications, which had speeded up police response to robberies and resulted in more criminals being caught in the act. These criminals were more likely to grab hostages in hopes of bargaining for their escape.

Eisendorfer and Schlossberg began drawing up some guidelines. From the start, the emphasis was on seeking nonviolent solutions to hostage situations, as opposed to the use of brute force. In their research, the two New York officers found that practically nothing had been written on the subject of negotiating for hostage release. They were starting from scratch.

They first analyzed the different types of hostage-takers and learned that they fell into three basic categories: the professional criminal whose escape is blocked during the commission of a crime; the psychotic; and the terrorist or fanatic promoting a cause or belief.

In working up their guidelines, Eisendorfer and Schlossberg had a primary objective—to save lives, not only those of the hostages but also of police and other law-enforcement officers and of the hostage-takers themselves. They searched for a way to ease anxieties and tensions in crisis situations, and the best way to do this, they decided, was through talk. The first positive step in any hostage negotiation is the opening up of a conversation between the person or persons holding the hostage and the law officers in charge.

Time is perhaps the most important single factor working for authorities in such crises. "As a general rule, the more time the felon spends with the hostage, the less likely he or she is to take the hostage's life, because each becomes acquainted and develops feelings for the other," Schlossberg says. He calls this a "positive transference of feelings." That is, he explains, you go on the assumption that it is harder for a person to kill someone he or she knows than to kill a total stranger. As we said earlier, this is known as the "Stockholm Syndrome."

Not only is it harder for the captors to kill people they have grown to know and, in some cases, like and respect, but also prolonged negotiations can give authorities time to locate a terrorist hideout. Once such a site has been pinpointed, the hostage-taker's bargaining position has been severely weakened. If police surround an apartment or a house where they know hostages are being held, the captors may give up demands, such as to free their comrades from a distant jail, in an effort to bargain for their own lives.

The more restricted the surroundings, the more desperate the situation. Take an aircraft hijacking, for example. Sooner or later, the plane must land, and unless it is refueled, it is stuck there. Or once on land the plane can be disabled. Its tires can be shot out.

Once this happens, the hostage-taker's plight worsens. The aircraft cabin can become extremely uncomfortable—either stiflingly hot or frigid, depending upon the weather outside. The air inside gets stale. Food supplies become exhausted. Toilets overflow. Passengers may become sick, and this is bad, both for the terrorists' morale and their public image.

Most often, terrorists pressed for time, in an effort to end their discomfort, or realizing how desperate their situation has become, lower their demands. This is precisely what happened to a skyjacked TWA airliner in 1976. Croatian terrorists had taken over the plane in New York, and it flew to Paris, France, where it landed. French police disabled the plane's landing gear.

Along the way, the skyjackers had released leaflets telling of their cause, and these had been aired on television, so at least some of their demands had already been met. By this time, negotiators knew the Croatians and their hostages were tired and worn out and ready to talk.

Negotiators told them the plane could not take off. They were stuck. If they killed any hostages or tried to make a run for it, police would shoot or capture them, and if they were caught by the French police, they very likely would be convicted and then executed. If, however, they gave themselves up to American authorities (since the plane had been taken over in the United States), they very likely would receive prison sentences and could be paroled in a few years. The terrorists thought it over and eventually surrendered to the American police.

Experts say that many hostage-takers, especially terrorists, proclaim their readiness to die for their cause, if necessary. But, in fact, this is more rhetoric than reality. It is the negotiator's job to talk them down from this point of view, to defuse a tense situation and then make the captors believe they will be able to get what they want, or at least a part of what they want, without having to die.

One way to encourage this to happen is simply to listen and be sympathetic. Another is to permit the hostage-takers to air their grievances publicly, on television and in the newspapers. Still another is to grant modest requests, such as for food, coffee, or cigarettes in exchange for minor concessions. In one instance involving a bank robber who held several people hostage in Silver Spring, Maryland, in 1977, the man asked for a six-pack of beer. An alert police sergeant acting as negotiator asked him what brand, in hopes of opening a conversation. The robber asked for Budweiser, and a fragile rapport was established when the sergeant sent him the beer in a swap for one of the hostages. Another hostage was traded for a submarine sandwich.[45]

"On our cases, we try talking, talking, and more talking. We try to bore them to death," says Lieutenant Francis Bolz, who heads the New York City Police Department's hostage-negotiating unit. Bolz is probably the most experienced officer in the nation, if not the world, in this highly specialized service. He says that a good deal of his and other negotiators' efforts involve common sense; negotiators must think quickly on their feet and adapt to sometimes fast-changing situations.

"There are certain sets of rules, however," he points out. "For one thing, you do not give weapons or ammunition to hostage takers. Also, you do not exchange prisoners. You never exchange a police officer for a hostage."[46]

Also, common to all hostage-negotiating teams, are the application of elementary psychology principles, like ignoring the hostage during the siege, both to show the hostage-taker that he or she is getting all the attention and because history has shown that hostages often become more intent on helping the gunman or terrorist than on securing their own release.

Bolz and other experts, such as Lieutenant Richard Klapp in San Francisco and Assistant Chief Rabe in Washington, D.C., prefer to have the negotiations handled exclusively by them or by other trained officers. They will rarely call in the wife, parents, or friends of a hostage-taker, especially if the hostage-taker is mentally disturbed. They have found that it is usually the actions of a relative or friend that has set this person off in the first place, and bringing him or her to the scene could trigger an explosive emotional reaction.

Bernie Thompson, one of the FBI's most experienced negotiators, believes the first half-hour or so of any hostage-holding incident is the most critical. "This is

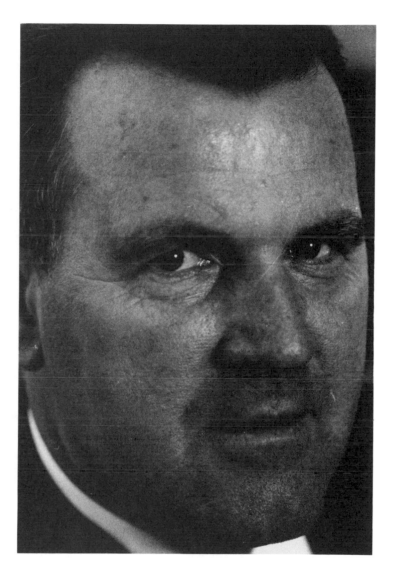

*Frank Bolz, a New York City
police negotiator, has helped
successfully end over eighty
hostage situations in his city.*

the time when criminals are most likely to act violently because they fear for their lives," Thompson says. "Everything is fever-pitched. It's not the time to press in any way. So you try to be low key, to defuse things from a panic state to a more stable one.

"You try to reassure the criminals that no one is going to rush in after them. Once they have been stabilized to the point they can be engaged in conversation and realize they have not been attacked or rushed," Thompson says, "the negotiator then attempts to establish trust between himself or herself and the hostage-taker. To accomplish this, you don't make false promises. You have to negotiate from a position of good faith. You're trying to establish credibility to convince the person you are sincere in what you are doing. If you misrepresent anything, it probably will come back to haunt you.

"I try to relate to the criminals as though they are people with dignity, people whose current problems have led them to what they feel are logical actions. I'm willing to hear out what their concerns are, to provide them with a way out, a way to save face. The last thing I want to do is to panic them, and I work on the assumption they will not take lives unless they're forced into it."

Schlossberg concurs. "All of these people holding hostages have problems of one kind or another," he says. "The key thing is to recognize this and not to close off all possible solutions to that problem.

"As long as there is some possibility of a solution, the person will work on the problem. But danger is present if the solution is foreclosed and homicide or suicide are the only options available."

Thompson says to avoid upsetting the hostage-taker, the negotiator must not say anything threatening or irritating. Lieutenant Bolz adds, "What we try to do in the talking is to change their thought patterns. If they say, for example, we want such and such a person—it may be a sworn enemy of the terrorist or the deranged person's wife—we change the subject. We may ask them if they need something to eat.

Bolz, Thompson, and others acknowledge that conversation, the more the better, is the key element in hostage negotiations. Such conversation not only serves to calm and stabilize the hostage-taker but also to wear him or her down.

What kind of person is best suited for hostage negotiations? First, only volunteers are selected. "It must be someone who is willing to do it," says Assistant Chief Rabe. "You need someone with a great deal of common sense for this type of job. Of course, you need to be able to converse well," Rabe adds, "but you need to be a good listener also, and sometimes that's more important than talking.

"You have to be flexible. You can't be rigid in negotiations. You have to be able to move in whichever direction the situation takes. You have to be fast thinking and able to analyze as you listen, so you can stay one step ahead. And very important, you have to handle pressure well. This is no spot for timid or nervous types."

"The essence of the negotiation process," says Lieutenant Klapp of the San Francisco Police Department, "is recognizing and effectively coping with the psychological trauma of the person in any such incident. Negotiators are selected on the basis of established performance as police officers, exceptional interpersonal skills, and demonstrated ability to defuse highly emotional conflicts."[47]

The FBI has developed its own training program on hostage negotiations, under the supervision of its Behavioral Science Unit. It has made this program available to numerous police departments throughout the United States and to law-enforcement agencies in Canada and Europe.

Many departments have taken the basic training program and refined it. In San Francisco and Washington, for example, hostage negotiators use role-playing. That is, they act out hostage scenes, with one officer playing the criminal, another the police negotiator, and others the hostages.

Although many of the negotiating principles developed in the United States are now commonly applied all over the world, some countries have developed their own methods of negotiating with hostage-takers. In Holland, for example, psychologists are used exclusively. When the South Moluccans hijacked a train there in 1975, one veteran psychologist spent hours analyzing the characters and emotional histories of the men and women held captive on the train. He was concerned that someone might challenge the Moluccans and thereby create a crisis.

In discussing negotiating with hostage-takers, Dutch expert Dr. Dick Mulder says: "They are like miners down below when there has been an accident. They need contact, the human voice, more than food. And you must give them room, time to discuss things, and think."[48]

In more recent years, as the wave of terrorist hostage-taking has spread through the Middle East, especially to Beirut, Lebanon, a new breed of negotiator has emerged. Typical of this genre is Terry Waite, a special envoy of the archbishop of Canterbury. On several occasions, he was called in to work out hostage-release agreements when all other efforts failed.

In 1981, he gained freedom for three Anglican missionaries accused of spying by Iranian officials. In 1985, he coaxed Libyan dictator Muammar Qadhaffi into freeing four English hostages who had been held for eight months, and later that year Waite's behind-the-scenes negotiations helped win the release of U.S. missionary Benjamin Weir, held captive for sixteen months by Shiite Moslem extremists.

*Terry Waite, special envoy to Lebanon of
the Archbishop Robert Runcie of Canterbury,
England, speaks to the press. He himself
has been missing since January 1987
and is presumed to have been taken hostage.*

How did Waite work? His wife, Frances, said, "he has enormous courage and a tremendous ability to get through to people of all kinds." Others said he truly understood how to deal with complex Mideast personalities. "He is quite able to sit down and drink coffee for a couple of days, doing nothing, and not get impatient," said Paul Oestreicher of the British Council of Churches. Also, Waite had no pronounced political view of his own and stressed that he represented a humanitarian church, not a government.[49] Waite himself was taken hostage in Beirut in January 1987, while he was negotiating for the release of two Americans. He is either dead or still being held captive—no one is certain which, since he has not been heard from since then.

Still another type of negotiator is represented by Nabih Berri, a Shiite Moslem Amal leader based in Beirut. Berri was instrumental in helping free Americans being held captive by a religious fanatic group in Lebanon after their TWA plane was hijacked in 1985. Berri has dealt in a number of such cases over the past few years and is effective, experts believe, because he understands the beliefs and causes of the radical terrorist groups now operating in the Middle East. He also has close contacts with many leaders in the area.

People such as Waite and Berri act as brokers or referees in hostage negotiations. Since they are not directly involved with either side, they can work objectively in trying to bring the captors and those trying to free the hostages together. In kidnappings by terrorists, it is these "middlemen" who often set the ground rules for negotiations.

Although the personalities, qualifications, and individual techniques of negotiators may vary from country to country, most experts agree that negotiations generally have proven to be the most successful way to effectively deal with hostage-takers. In the United States and Canada, for example, hundreds of cities and communitics have hostage-negotiating teams professionally prepared to deal with any emergency.

"Over the years, the New York City Police Department hostage negotiation team has done well in excess of six hundred jobs," says Schlossberg. "We haven't lost a hostage or a policeman or a perpetrator since the negotiations got underway."

No lives have been lost in San Francisco either since Lieutenant Klapp's team has been in operation. "Those of us involved in hostage negotiation," he says, "are deeply committed to the concept. We feel that it has added a new dimension to [our] ability to deal effectively with the most violent situations."

Bernie Thompson and Patrick Mullany of the FBI believe that in a democracy, hostage-takers must be negotiated with—not because of their rights but because of the rights of their victims, the hostages.

"Negotiation is the most compassionate, most humane, and most professional way to handle crisis situations," says Lieutenant Klapp. "We know that we have saved lives and that is the way we know we have to go."[50]

This view was supported in a 1977 U.S. government task force report on coping with terror and civil disorders. The report acknowledged the deadly power of a person with a gun and a group of hostages over the rest of society, calling it a strength equal to "his or her own ruthlessness, recklessness, or the extent of his or her mental derangement." It also acknowledged the dilemma for authorities who are torn between preserving life and giving in to terror. Even so, the report still recommended persuasion over force, saying, "Society should aim to outwit the terrorist rather than to outfight him."[51]

CHAPTER THIRTEEN

THE MEDIA INFLUENCE

It is a phenomenon of our technological times that the international media, especially television, plays an important, if at times unwitting, role in modern-era hostage-taking. One of the key objectives of terrorists is to communicate their message to as broad an audience as possible, and what better way is there than TV and radio? Via satellite, they can be heard around the world.

Almost every major hostage-taking incident of the past twenty years has been "front-page news" to the media. Hostage-taking has received a tremendous amount of coverage. Aldo Moro, the *Achille Lauro*, the hijacking of TWA airliners—all were on newscasts for days and weeks. Even during the Iranian hostage case, which lasted well over a year, hardly a day went by without some media reminder.

To the media, hostages, especially if they have recognizable names, are big news. As the old expression goes, such news "sells papers." In fact, during prolonged instances involving terrorists and captives, there is fierce competition among the media to get exclusive stories on what is happening. Television networks go to great lengths to get interviews with both those who kidnap and their victims.

All of this is, of course, exactly what the captors seek—attention. It gives them a perfect medium to express their views—to damn a government and its leaders or to call notice to perceived or real injustices to their beliefs.

Says author Walter Laqueur, an expert on terrorism: "Guerrilla warfare can exist without media coverage, but for terrorism, publicity is absolutely essential, and the smaller the terrorist gang, the more it depends on publicity."[52] Laqueur notes that terrorism in dictatorships goes unreported, but in democratic societies, journalists have almost unrestricted access. Consequently, constant, detailed coverage, even of relatively unimportant events gets blown out of proportion, giving terrorism more significance than perhaps it deserves.

For example, he says, hostage events usually involving small numbers of people make for bigger stories than the killing of thousands in the Iran-Iraq war, in Afghanistan, in Cambodia, and in the Ugandan civil war. Conversely, the 1985 Beirut hostage crisis, in which a few Americans aboard a TWA flight were held captive by hijackers, drew blanket coverage for weeks, especially from U.S. networks. Up to two-thirds of the nightly half-hour newscasts were devoted to the hostages and their captors.

In some instances, experts point out, the media—again primarily the major U.S. TV networks—have actually paid the terrorists for rights to cover a hostage situation. In the 1985 TWA hijacking, for instance, it is alleged that the networks paid over $1 million a week to assure their monopoly of live coverage. Up to $50,000 each was paid for tapes of hostage interviews, which obviously were staged to make the captors appear as sympathetic figures. Hostages later said they were forced by the terrorists to make the statements they did on the tapes, and many of them, in fact, said they bitterly resented the media saturation and sometimes favorable coverage television afforded their captors.

Some experts believe that such publicity may actually encourage even more cases of hostage-taking. Vice-President George Bush's Task Force, in its Public Report, had this to say: "Among the factors cited for the increases in both the number and sensational nature of incidents is the terrorists' success in achieving wider publicity and influencing a much broader audience. Terrorists see the media's role in conveying their messages worldwide as essential to achieving their goals. If the violence is spectacular, wide coverage is usually assured."[53]

Laqueur agrees. "Most investigations," he has written, "have shown that there is some correlation between coverage by the media, above all television, and the spread of terrorism, specifically hijackings and assassinations. The most serious effect of media reporting on terrorism is the likely increase of terroristic activities. The media can provide the potential terrorists with all the ingredients that are necessary to engage in this type of violence.

"The overall effect of the relationship between the media and terrorism has been the exaggeration of the importance of terrorism, and its embellishment."

Laqueur also says that the media can build up terrorists from virtually unknown status to the point where they become highly recognizable world figures. He cites the case of Libya's Qadhaffi as a classic example. "Never before," he says, "had a person of so little consequence been built up into a demonic figure threatening all mankind; never had a little man who was obviously not quite stable been transformed into a superhuman figure and been taken so seriously. Future historians may find it inexplicable how TV turned low comedy into high drama."[54]

Many contend that widespread media coverage can greatly aid terrorists in a number of ways. It can limit or preempt a government's options in dealing with the case. It airs terrorist propaganda and gives coverage to obviously staged events. If hostage-takers learn through media coverage that authorities are closing in on their hideout, they can move, always staying a step ahead of detection.

Laqueur says that there have been many instances in which media coverage either directly helped terrorism or contributed to the prolongation of a crisis. He cites the Iranian hostage situation, saying, "only after the last ounce of publicity had been squeezed out by the captors were the hostages released."

One area where the press has its own "conscience" problem is when terrorists demand coverage. In free societies, the media does not like to be told what they can or can't print or televise. But there have been a number of cases where terrorists have warned that unless their demands are aired, hostages would be killed. At times, this may mean giving exposure to the rantings of disturbed people. But if the media does not comply, this could risk the lives of those being held. In most cases, to date, coverage has been afforded.

This was dramatically exemplified in February 1975 when terrorists kidnapped German politician Peter Lorenz and asked in exchange for sparing his life the release of five of their comrades in prison. For three days, television closely covered this crisis.

One TV editor later commented: "For 72 hours we just lost control of the medium. We shifted shows to meet their timetable. Our cameras had to be in position to record each of the prisoners [after their release] as they boarded the plane, and our news coverage had to include prepared statements at their dictation. There is plenty of underworld crime on our screens, but up until now Kojak and Columbo were always in charge. Now it was the real thing, and it was the gangsters who wrote the scripts and programmed the mass media."[55]

All of this has created a huge controversy: Should the media cover such events, and if so, how much coverage should be given?

Editors, reporters, and broadcast executives stoutly argue that a hostage-taking event, like war, disasters, or anything else, is news, and the public has a right to know. As to hindering the search for where terrorists are holding hostages, the media says that if airing such information is harmful to the goals of the authorities, they will keep it secret.

"Terrorist acts are newsworthy," says the Bush report, "and the media see coverage as a professional, competitive responsibility. Some in the media have claimed that intense coverage helps to resolve an incident and that putting the hostages on television may actually save their lives. The other side of this argument is that untimely or inaccurate information released by the media can interfere with resolution of an incident, foreclose options for dealing with it, or unwittingly provide intelligence information to terrorists, which prolongs an incident or endangers lives.

"The solution to these problems is not government-imposed restraint that conflicts with the First Amendment's protection of freedom of speech and the press. The media must serve as their own watchdog. Journalistic guidelines have been developed for use during wartime to protect lives and national security, and in some circumstances should be considered appropriate during a terrorist situation."[56]

The Bush report also cites the fact that many Americans believe terrorists use the media to achieve their goals. Experts also feel that the U.S. media, and again television networks in particular, give far more coverage to terrorist events than do other media representatives around the world.

This has led to some interesting side effects. When so much coverage was given to the airline and ship hijackings in the mid-1980s in the U.S. media, tens of thousands of American tourists canceled vacation trips to Europe and the Middle East. Yet Europeans and others continued as usual to take their holidays in those areas of the world.

The Bush Task Force also reported that much of the U.S. media coverage concentrates on the families of hostages. They make for good human-interest stories. "The public statements understandably reflect the perspectives of distraught individuals principally concerned with the safe return of their relatives. Some of these statements may unintentionally play into the hands of terrorists, who reinforce the families' concerns by claiming the lives of the hostages are in danger. Family members sometimes turn to the media to bring pressure on the administration to take action that may not be appropriate or possible."

In conclusion, the Bush report recommended the following: "News coverage of terrorism has created a dilemma for media executives: how to keep the people informed without compromising public security. Solving this problem will have to be a joint effort between media and government representatives.

"The government must improve its communications with the media during a terrorist attack. At the same time, the media must maintain high standards of reporting to ensure that the lives of innocent victims and national security are not jeopardized."[57]

CHAPTER FOURTEEN

A CONFUSION
OF POLICIES

The official U.S. government policy regarding hostages held by terrorist groups, like the policies of many other nations around the world, has flip-flopped back and forth over the years. For fifteen years or more, the United States held reasonably tight to a hard-line policy that called for no bargaining whatsoever with terrorist groups. This policy was initiated in the late 1960s by President Richard Nixon, when the Tupamaros in Uruguay kidnapped former U.S. official Dan Mitrione. Nixon said that the United States would make no deals with the rebels of any nation. Mitrione was subsequently killed by the Tupamaros, but this did not change American policy.[58] When hostage-taking and the bombing of U.S. facilities increased in the early 1970s, Nixon asked Congress for, and got, more than $20 million in appropriations to add extra protection for U.S. missions and embassies in other countries.

But the U.S. hard line eased somewhat during the Carter presidency in the late 1970s. This was spotlighted by the capture and holding of the American hostages in

Iran. Carter did agree to the abortive rescue mission, but other than that he opted for a "wait and see" position that many critics felt showed the country as being weak and indecisive.

One of the harshest critics of this position at the time was Ronald Reagan, then a candidate for president. Speaking of the Iran hostage situation in February 1980, Reagan said, "There comes a time when a government has got to be willing to set a date for their [the hostages] release and let them [those taking hostages] know privately what the option will be if they [hostages] are not released. . . . We should have done it back about the end of the first or second week that they were held."

A year later, as he welcomed home the Iranian hostages, President Reagan added, "Let terrorists be aware that when the rules of international behavior are violated, our policy will be one of swift and effective retribution."[59]

Others in Reagan's administration echoed the tough-policy stand. In 1984, for example, Secretary of State George Shultz said, "Terrorism is aggression, and, like all aggression, must be forcefully resisted. The public must understand there is a potential for a loss of life of some of our fighting men and the loss of life of some innocent people."

A year later, in early 1985, Reagan spoke again on the subject, saying, "Terrorists and those who support them must, and will, be held to account. None of us, any country, can afford to pay off terrorists." And, on another occasion, he said, "America will never make concessions to terrorists. To do so would only invite more terrorism."

During this period, Reagan sought commitment from friendly countries to take a number of positive measures against those who encouraged the kidnappings. He asked for uniformly tough security measures at airports around the world. He asked Congress to approve a budget request for $3.5 billion over a five-year period to reconstruct or relocate 126 diplomatic missions overseas and to create a security service that would guard against terrorist attacks. He also called for measures to protect against electronic eavesdropping on U.S. embassies in an attempt to cut off the flow of sensitive information available to potential terrorists.

Reagan also suggested a trade boycott of nations that continue to promote terrorism. This suggestion, however, brought only lukewarm support, especially from allies who depended upon such countries for oil.

In time, though, Reagan learned as so many other leaders had before him, that it is one thing to talk tough and quite another to act that way. He had called for swift retaliation against those who abducted U.S. hostages, but when Lebanese radicals kidnapped hostages aboard a TWA flight in mid-1985 and held them prisoner for weeks, Reagan softened his stance.

"I could get mad enough now to think of a couple of things we could do to retaliate, but I would probably be sentencing a number of Americans to death if I did it," he said. "I have to wait it out as long as these people are there, threatened and alive, and we have a possibility of bringing them home."[60]

So, one might ask, was his position any different from that of President Carter's during the Iranian hostage crisis? Not really, it would seem. *U.S. News & World Report* said that Reagan was "confronted with a growing perception of America as victim, helpless to protect its citizens abroad and powerless to react. Hostages were being held on foreign shores, their families at home worry-stricken. The bodies of still more Americans were being sent back."[61]

In April 1986, President Reagan suddenly took a more dramatic stand against terrorism. He authorized a retaliatory strike against Colonel Muammar Qadhaffi, the Libyan leader, who had long been suspected of supporting international terrorist groups. U.S. intelligence sources had directly linked Qadhaffi with terrorists who had killed dozens of people in shootings at Rome and Vienna airports and with bombings at U.S. military bases in Europe.

The strike consisted of an air raid in which thirteen F-111 fighter-bombers and twelve A-6 attack planes blasted military and intelligence targets in and around Tripoli, Libya's capital, and the coastal city of Benghazi. Each F-111 carried sixteen 2,000-pound (900-kg) bombs. Damage to the primary targets, including the Bab al Azizia barracks and the living quarters and command center of Qadhaffi himself, was extensive. More than thirty Libyans were killed, reportedly including the eighteen-month-old adopted daughter of Qadhaffi.

Time magazine, in reporting the attack, said: "The U.S. launched its bombers out of a grim conviction that ruthless attacks on Americans and citizens of many other nations will never let up until terrorists and the states that sponsor them are made to pay a price in kind."[62]

Addressing the country on television following the raid, President Reagan said, "the air strike will not only diminish Colonel Gadaffi's [Qadhaffi's] capacity to export terror, it will provide him with incentives and reasons to alter his criminal behavior."[63]

Reagan added: "We have done what we had to do. If necessary, we shall do it again. The United States won but a single engagement in the long battle against terrorism."

Secretary of Defense Caspar Weinberger, generally known for being against reprisals, backed Reagan on the justification for the bombing raid on Libya. "Terrorism is now a state-practiced activity, a method of waging war," he said. "It will get steadily worse unless the U.S. convinces terrorists otherwise." Most of the American public also approved of the action. In a national poll, more than 70 percent said they favored the retaliatory strike.

But world opinion was strongly against the raid. Italian Prime Minister Bettino Craxi expressed the concerns of European governments and citizens alike. The U.S. action, he said, "was likely to unleash explosions of fanaticism and of criminal and suicide missions."[64]

This did not happen. Although there were a few minor incidents and torrents of threatening words from Qadhaffi in the months that followed the bombing, there were no major terrorist attacks in Europe. Whether or not this was pure coincidence, or whether the bombing run had the direct effect of deterrence, is difficult to determine.

CHAPTER FIFTEEN

ARMS FOR HOSTAGES

As the kidnappings of more and more Americans continued in Lebanon in the mid-1980s, President Reagan began to show the strain of an anguished administration that seemed able to do little in response, despite all the tough talk aimed at terrorists. When three more Americans were taken hostage in early 1987, *Newsweek* magazine summed up the presidential dilemma by saying, " . . . Reagan could do nothing stronger to retaliate than put the country off limits to U.S. citizens."

The president himself said at the time, "There is a limit to what our government can do for Americans in a chaotic situation such as that in Lebanon today." The U.S. government banned travel to Lebanon by most holders of American passports, and it ordered about 1,500 U.S. citizens still living there to leave within thirty days.[65]

But this was indeed a weak response in light of Reagan's past threats and actions. The Reagan administration felt as so many other leaders had before it, frustrated and helpless.

] 119 [

Soon after this, however, some startling revelations surfaced about U.S. policies regarding hostages. These revelations shocked the nation, exposing the administration as saying one thing publicly and doing exactly the opposite secretly.

The first damaging disclosure came in May 1987, when Robert McFarlane, former national security advisor to Reagan, testified before U.S. Senate and House of Representatives committees in Washington. McFarlane said the president, despite pledging publicly never to yield to terrorist demands, had, behind the scenes, approved a scheme to ransom two Americans being held hostage in Lebanon with $2 million in private funds. "It involved no government funds," McFarlane testified, "but it did involve bribes of guards and people in the chain from the immediate housing of the prisoners to their ultimate escape from Lebanon." This particular plot fell through, but the American public nevertheless was dismayed that Reagan would okay such a plan. And, shortly after this, the Iran-Contra arms scandal broke, causing the president to lose an enormous amount of credibility with the American people. This story, of course, made front-page and prime-time television news for months as it unfolded.

Reagan had approved a deal in 1986 to sell weapons to Iran in exchange for the release of American hostages in Lebanon. Monies received from the arms sales were to be given to the Nicaraguan Contras to help them in their fight to overthrow the Sandinista government in power in Nicaragua (see Chapter 9).

All of this was being done without the knowledge or approval of the U.S. Congress. In fact, Congress had officially cut off aid to the Contras.

The most devastating testimony came from Rear Admiral John Poindexter, another former Reagan national security advisor. In July 1987, he told a congressional investigating committee that President Reagan had signed an order in 1985 authorizing weapons shipments to Iran for the express purpose of swapping arms for hostages. Poindexter also said that in October 1986, he had obtained the approval of the president for a nine-point proposal between American businessman Albert Hakim and Iranian officials that provided the basis for the last arms-for-hostages deal. The agreement included a plan for the release of seventeen Lebanese terrorists held in a Kuwaiti prison—a position in clear violation of stated U.S. policy.

Reagan, for a while, insisted that the arms sales to Iran were not expressly for the release of American hostages. The deals were made, he said, in an effort to better U.S. relations with Iran. But later, in a national speech, he admitted the whole episode "was a mistake."

Reagan said, "A few months ago I told the American people I did not trade arms for hostages. My heart and my best intentions still tell me that is true, but the facts and evidence tell me it is not." Then, addressing the families of American hostages in Lebanon, he added, "We have not given up. We never will. And I promise you we'll use every legitimate means to free your loved ones from captivity."[66]

Not only did these covert events bring to light the confusion and frustration of the Reagan administration in finding an effective way to deal with the hostage situation, but they also rocked the nation, greatly tarnishing the once-popular image of the president.

A special commission looking into the Iran-Contra affair, headed by former U.S. Senator John Tower of Texas, rebuked Reagan in its report, which said that the president's decision to sell arms to Iran "rewarded a regime that clearly supported terrorism and hostage taking." The *Washington Post*, in a front-page editorial, said: "President Reagan's deep obsession with Americans held hostage in Lebanon became the animating spirit behind the clandestine arms shipment. Reagan swept aside all cautionary warnings and personally pushed the initiative despite repeated failures.

"The United States allowed itself to be utterly bamboozled by Iran. Tehran repeatedly flaunted its bad faith by promising more hostage releases than it ever delivered; the Americans seemed to repay the Iranians' unreliability with greater trust and more missiles. Some of the most senior officials of the U.S. government, including the director of the Central Intelligence Agency and two national security advisors, showed a persistent gullibility in dealing with the Iranians."[67]

The exposé of the Iranian arms-hostage scandal also left U.S. policy regarding hostages in a shambles. Robert McFarlane said that attempting to trade arms for hostages made the United States vulnerable to new kidnappings. *Newsweek* magazine proved McFarlane's warning to be accurate when, in February 1987, it pointed out that more Americans were prisoners [in Lebanon] now than when Reagan began his negotiations with the Iranian government. As *Newsweek* stated, "Facing its limits, Washington [the Reagan administration] may have to acknowledge that there are times when a great power cannot prevent itself from being kicked around by a smaller one."[68]

CHAPTER SIXTEEN

SEARCHING FOR
A SOLUTION

Is there a satisfactory solution to terrorism and hostage-taking? If so, what is it?

Robert Oakley, who runs the U.S. State Department's antiterrorism program, sees no easy answers. He says, "Responses from governments to terrorist attacks will tend to ebb and flow. Terrorism will not easily disappear."[69]

One leading authority who believes terrorism can be stopped is Benjamin Netanyahu, Israel's ambassador to the United Nations. A former soldier, he is also the brother of Lieutenant Colonel Jonathan Netanyahu, who was killed while leading the successful Israeli raid to free hostages at Entebbe, Uganda, in 1976. He has written and lectured extensively on how best to deal with terrorism and hostage-taking.

Netanyahu believes resolutely in a strong position of no concessions whatsoever to terrorist demands, backed by the liberal use of force in retaliation. He says, for example, that terrorists generally fear military intervention and that this fear has a tremendously inhibiting effect on hostage-taking.

To prove his point, he cites the large number of instances when Israeli hostages were taken in the 1970s. In all cases the country refused to give in to the captors' demands, and in a majority of cases, soldiers overcame the terrorists and liberated the hostages.

Netanyahu says this type of tough policy can, at times, cause painful consequences. When Israeli troops raided terrorists holding school children at Ma'alot in 1974, twenty-one of the children were massacred before the terrorists were killed. But, he adds, the policy worked overall, because hostage-taking became a rarity in Israel.

One reason it has worked, Netanyahu contends, is that contrary to popular myth, suicidal terrorists are rare. Terrorists, overwhelmingly, not only want to live but want to escape unpunished.

He says that when other countries have followed Israel's example of applying force rather than conceding to terrorist demands, hostage-taking incidents decreased, particularly in Great Britain and West Germany.

In fact, military force is the cornerstone of a three-pronged strategy Netanyahu proposes to halt terrorism. He points to the successes of the U.S. seizure of the *Achille Lauro* hijackers and the U.S. bombing of Libyan bases after it was proven that Libya's Qadhaffi was supporting international terrorism. Qadhaffi, who had threatened military reprisals if ever attacked, instead retreated into defeated silence.

Netanyahu says that military action should be supported by economic and political pressures against countries such as Libya and Iran,which are known to support terrorism and hostage-taking. He suggests boycotts and embargos of products going into and out of these nations, as well as the closing of embassies and the cutting off of diplomatic relations.

But, he believes, such sanctions coupled with military action can only work if all affected countries cooperate. "What is required," he has written, "is a basic realignment of international attitudes toward terrorism. Governments must be made to understand that if they give in to terrorism, they are in practice supporting it."[70]

In short, he has said: " A policy of firmness will make it clear that individual terrorists will be pursued, caught and punished; that organizations that launch them will be subject to attack; that governments that shelter them will face political, economic and, ultimately, military retaliation."

Netanyahu says that enforcing such a policy will require courage and may involve great risks, and if hostages are occasionally killed, government leaders will face public criticism. But he and many other experts sincerely believe that such a strategy is the only way to rid the world of terrorism. Anything less will only continue to encourage it.

One such expert who agrees, particularly on the policy of military retaliation, is Lawrence Eagleburger, former U.S. undersecretary of state. He says the United States owes its citizens—here or in any other part of the world—protection to the degree it can give it. "Retaliation," he has said, "would make it clear to everybody that Americans abroad are nobody's free targets." He also feels that the United States has an obligation to American citizens in places where courts of law cannot reach. "My conviction is that we will save a lot more lives in the long run by being tough and steady," he says.[71]

James Schlesinger, former U.S. secretary of defense, believes what is needed is the ability to "bust up" terrorist organizations. He has said, "the purpose of [a military retaliatory] operation should be to destroy the power of a terrorist organization. Most important . . . is for [the United States] to establish a pattern of behavior on which other nations will base their expectations. It is important for others to have a high level of expectation that the perpetrators of terrorist acts will be punished. The character of the punishment matters a lot less than the certainty that they will be punished. This means establishing a pattern over a period of years. It means avoiding sending conflicting signals. It means not issuing threats and then backing off. If you make a threat and then don't deliver, that raises morale and whets the appetite on the other side."[72]

One expert who agrees with Schlesinger is James Adams, author of *The Financing of Terror*. Adams says, "The Western alliance has so far demonstrated a striking lack of united resolve in the face of terrorism. Rather than coordinating policy to meet the threat, it has continued to try to counter terrorism on national lines. Terrorists can flee France to find sanctuary across the border in Belgium, leave Ulster (Northern Ireland) and find a home in the U.S. Even when agreements have been reached, their implementation has been arbitrary.

"At the same time," Adams points out, "those nations which support terrorism, such as Libya, Iran, and Syria, can do so without the allies reaching an agreement which would make such support of terrorism too expensive to bear, both economically and politically.

"There is no quick and easy solution to the terrorist problem. Occasional short-term gains, while politically satisfying, must be sacrificed to achieve longer term benefits, which will do more to undercut the structure of international terrorism.

"The key," summarizes Adams, "is not military action, but better intelligence gathering, including the infiltration of terrorist groups, the sharing of information among the Western allies, and a common policy to counter the growing threat."[73]

What, then, is the ultimate solution to terrorism and hostage-taking? One thing seems clear. The solution will not be found until all civilized nations fully recognize the problem and lay aside their personal national interests in a united effort to solve it.

Thus, to be successful in effectively curbing terrorism worldwide requires a truly international effort. This was one of the conclusions of Vice-President Bush's Task Force. "More and more states recognize that unilateral programs for combatting terrorism are not sufficient," the report stated. "Without a viable, comprehensive, cooperative effort, terrorism and its supporters will benefit from the uncoordinated actions of its victims. International cooperation alone cannot eliminate terrorism, but it can complicate the terrorists' tasks, deter their efforts, and save lives."[74]

The United States is already working closely with such nations as Canada, the United Kingdom, France, West Germany, Italy, and Japan. It also is looking for ways in which it can cooperate more closely with other nations.

According to the Bush report, substantial progress in international cooperation has been made in such areas as aviation and maritime security. For example, in June 1985, following the hijacking of TWA flight 847, the International Civil Aviation Organization moved quickly to upgrade its standards and recommended practices for airport and aircraft security. And, in November 1985, following the hijacking of the *Achille Lauro*, the International Maritime Organization, acting on a U.S. initiative, directed its Maritime Safety Committee to develop, on a priority basis, measures for the protection of passengers and crews aboard ships.

Says L. Paul Bremer, III, U.S. ambassador at large for counterterrorism: "Ten years ago, the terrorists seemed to have the initiative. They attacked or hijacked seemingly at will. In the mid-1980s, there has been an important shift in emphasis in the fight against terrorism. Now our fellow democracies are banding together and cooperating.

"The United States has worked with like-minded nations to develop multi-lateral agreements and declarations about terrorist attacks on civil aviation, internationally protected persons, passengerliners and hostage taking," says Bremer. "These documents reflect an important degree of agreement in principle where there was none a decade ago. I find a new sense of resolve about terrorism."[75]

Today, the United States follows a three-part strategy for dealing with terrorism. The first element is a policy of firmness toward terrorists. Says Bremer: "Giving in to terrorist demands will only breed future demands, demands which are likely to be greater than those of today. While the Iran-Contra affair may have caused some to doubt our steadfastness in resisting terrorist demands, I can assure you that there is no sense in the counterterrorism community that we should change our policy. No country, no terrorist should believe that there is anything to be gained by threatening the United States with terrorist action. We will not make concessions. We will not deal."

The second element of the national strategy, Bremer says, consists of practical measures to bring terrorists to justice. This includes the identification, tracking, apprehension, prosecution, and punishment of terrorists. In the past two years, more and more terrorists have been tried and jailed around the world, usually after receiving the kind of stiff sentences which were unheard of only a few years ago.[76]

The third element of the U.S. antiterrorism policy concerns putting pressure on terror-supporting states. For example, consider the U.S. sanctions against Libya over the past few years. Libya has been on the U.S. government's list of terror-supporting states since the list was first published in 1979.

Specifically, in the past decade, the United States has:

- closed its embassy in Libya and ordered the Libyan embassy in Washington closed;
- imposed harsh economic restrictions on Libya and strongly encouraged allies to take like action (the Europeans, in particular, have imposed political, diplomatic, and economic restraints on Libya);
- used military force, such as the air strikes on Libya's capital.

Syria, too, is a charter member on the list of terror-supporting states. Although Syria has long been involved in terrorism, it was especially active from 1983 to 1986, when Syria sponsored the Abu Nidal organization in a series of attacks on Jordan.

The revelation of Syria's direct role in a broad number of terrorist activities led to a series of responsive actions in late 1986 by the United Kingdom, the European community, and the United States. The United Kingdom broke off diplomatic relations with Syria. The United States withdrew its ambassador to Syria and imposed economic sanctions.

Virtually since it came to power a few years ago, the current regime in Iran has used terrorism, largely against U.S. and European targets, as well as moderate Arab states. The United States has taken an increasingly tough position toward Iran in response to its continuing support for terrorism. After Iran-backed radical groups bombed the U.S. embassy buildings and the Marine barracks in Lebanon in the 1980s, the United States placed Iran on the list of countries supporting international terrorism.

- The U.S. specifically has banned the export to Iran of a variety of items and equipment that could support terrorist and/or military operations, including helicopter and other aircraft, outboard engines, chemical weapons, and several other controlled items.

- The U.S. has encouraged its allies to also take action against Iran, and recently there has been increasing international pressure brought to bear demanding that Iran discontinue its sponsorship of terrorism.

In another area of international cooperation, the United States, Britain, Switzerland, Australia, and other states such as the Cayman Islands and the Turks and Caicos Islands, have agreed to a treaty that should help limit the flow of funds to terrorist groups. It allows access to the personal and corporate bank accounts of any person or company in these countries suspected of backing terrorism.

Many nations, particularly the United States and the Western European states, also are sharing high-tech intelligence information via sophisticated computer networks. The goal is for a counterterrorist expert in Washington to someday be able to use his or her computer to draw freely from the data bases of computers in other nations for information on international terrorist groups. The U.S. intelligence community is already busy installing a new computer system that will allow for the automatic analysis of thousands of files on terrorists—their operations, known contacts and resources.

Are such actions and sanctions against terror-supporting states working? Yes, says Bremer. "This policy has worked," he noted in his report to Congress. "While other nations have been slower to respond, today Libya is politically isolated. During the past year [1987] Libyan-supported terrorist operations have declined, although Qadhaffi still appears ready to use terrorism as a policy tool.

"Syria proved most sensitive to the political and diplomatic isolation. In June [1987], Syria expelled most of the Abu Nidal [terrorist] organization, and we have not seen evidence recently of Syrian involvement in terrorism. There are encouraging signs. Still, we intend to keep our remaining sanctions in place and to leave Syria on the list of terror-supporting states until we see evidence of a fundamental change in Syrian policy toward terrorism."

With regard to Iran, Bremer reported, "It has been under little concerted international pressure until recently, but is now increasingly isolated. Other countries have been reluctant to sever profitable commercial dealings, particularly in the absence of international cooperation. However, Iran's outrageous behavior is beginning to exact a toll with other countries."

Bremer says the ever-expanding circle of targets for terrorist attack, perhaps more than anything, has brought about a change in the international attitude toward dealing with the problem. "People and governments began to realize that terrorists could and would attack anyone. Here in America, the taking of our Tehran embassy catalyzed public opinion and led to demands for effective government action.

"The fact is, although terrorism continues around the world, one is much more likely these days to read news stories about terrorist arrests than about sensational hijackings. And gripping news accounts of terrorist atrocities have quietly given way to brief reports from Western capitals on the successful apprehension, prosecution, and punishment of terrorists," Bremer says.

As specific examples, he points out that from 1981 to 1985, international terrorism grew from some 500 incidents per year to about 800 incidents. But in 1986, terrorism dropped 6 percent, and there was another 10 percent decline in 1987. Also, contrary to the impression many Americans have, terrorism in Europe has dropped dramatically, by nearly one-third over the past three years. Additionally, in 1986, there were only two airline hijackings, the lowest number since records began to be kept more than twenty years ago.

In summarizing the long-term goal of the United States and other nations, Bremer says: "The West's strategic objective must be to reduce terrorism to a level at which it no longer dominates world policy. We can achieve this objective with a firm, concerted counter-terrorism effort sustained over 5 to 7 years. How? By making the general political, economic, and psychological climate in which terrorists operate more hostile. The targets of any counterterrorist measure, therefore, are not particular terrorists or groups, but the community of nations and the overall political environment.

"We had to get away from the defensive, muddled reaction to terrorist violence of the early 1970s and reassert, clearly and decisively, democracy's willingness to fight terrorism. We had to shift the public debate on terrorism from understanding 'root causes' to condemning the crimes terrorists commit."

Bremer is optimistic that the continuing fight against terrorism and hostage-taking is showing positive signs. "Around the world," he said in his concluding remarks to Congress in October 1987, "there is a cooperative spirit which we have not seen before. After nearly 20 years of disarray in the face of terrorism, the West is beginning to unite to confront terrorists as criminals.

"I do not want to leave the impression that our problems are solved, that there are not disagreements among friends, or that we will not suffer reverses in the months ahead. I do believe that the progress we are making is real, substantive, and permanent. We are not going to eliminate terrorism, but we are making the world a more dangerous place for terrorists and safer for the rest of us."[77]

NOTES

1. "You Can Run, But You Can't Hide," *Newsweek*, October 21, 1985, pp. 22–30.
2. James Adams, *The Financing of Terror* (New York: Simon & Schuster, 1987), p. 6.
3. Walter Laqueur, *The Age of Terrorism* (New York: Little, Brown, 1987), p. 11.
4. Adams, p. 10.
5. George Bush, *Public Report of the Vice President: Task Force on Combatting Terrorism* (Washington, D.C.: U.S. Government Printing Office, 1986), p. 1.
6. *Ibid.*, p. 1.
7. Laqueur, p. 78.
8. Bush, p. 2.
9. *Ibid.*, p. 2.
10. Paul Bremer, *Counterterrorism: U.S. Policy and Proposed Legislation*, U.S. Department of State Bulletin (January 1988), p. 45.
11. *Ibid.*, p. 51.
12. Bush, p. 3.
13. "Moscow's Invisible War of Terror Inside Pakistan," *Washington Post* (March 13, 1988), pp. C1–C4.
14. *Ibid.*, p. 4.
15. Caroline Moorehead, *Hostages to Fortune* (New York: Atheneum,), pp. 6–10.
16. *Ibid.*, p. 120.

17. *Ibid.*, p. 113.
18. William Schreiber, *The Ultimate Weapon: Terrorists & World Order* (New York: William Morrow & Co., 1978), p. 31.
19. Moorehead, p. 13.
20. *Ibid.*, p. 132.
21. *Ibid.*, p. 154.
22. "Seizing Hostages, Scourge of the '70s," *Newsweek* (March 21, 1977), p. 16.
23. "Murder on the Milk Train," *Time* (December 15, 1975), p. 25.
24. Moorehead, *Hostages to Fortune*, p. 172.
25. David Hubbard, *Winning Back the Sky* (Dallas: Saybrook Publishers, 1979), p. 44.
26. "Mideast Terror Strikes Americans," *U.S. News & World Report* (June 24, 1985), p. 9.
27. Rocky Sickmann, *Iranian Hostage—A Personal History* (N.C.: Crawford Press, 1982), pp. 8–9.
28. "Iran Plays the Hostage Game," *Newsweek* (February 9, 1987), pp. 34–36.
29. "Mideast Terror Strikes Americans," p. 9.
30. "Kidnapped in Beirut," *Reader's Digest* (April 1988), pp. 90–97.
31. "Hostage Release," *Time* (August 10, 1986), pp. 16–18.
32. Moorehead, *Hostages to Fortune*, p. 208.
33. *Ibid.*, p. 204.
34. Sickmann, *Iranian Hostage—A Personal History*, p. 15.
35. "Hostage Offer Refused," *Newport News Daily Press* (June 22, 1987), p. 1.
36. Moorehead, p. 202.
37. "My Hostage Life in Beirut Was Waiting and Praying," *Washington Post* (March 7, 1987), p. B1.
38. Moorehead, p. 213.
39. "Hostages: Living in the Aftermath," *U.S. News & World Report* (July 8, 1985), p. 34.
40. *Ibid.*, p. 34.
41. "A Cry From the 'Other' Hostages," *U.S. News & World Report* (September 29, 1986), p. 12.
42. "How the Israelis Pulled It Off," *Newsweek* (July 19, 1976), pp. 42–46; "The Countdown in Uganda," *Newsweek* (July 12, 1976), pp. 28–29; "Terrorism—How the West Can Win," *Reader's Digest* (July 1986), pp. 122–128.
43. "How the Israelis Pulled It Off," *Newsweek*, pp. 42–46.
44. "Horror and Death at the Olympics," *Time* (September 18, 1972), pp. 22–27.
45. "Seizing Hostages, Scourge of the '70s," *Newsweek* (March 21, 1977), p. 26.

46. L. B. Taylor, *Emergency Squads* (New York: Franklin Watts, 1980), p. 74.
47. *Ibid.*, p. 76.
48. Moorehead, p. 241.
49. "Hostage Negotiator Who Stands Tall," *U.S. News & World Report* (November 25, 1985), p. 13.
50. Taylor, *Emergency Squads*, p. 79.
51. *U.S. Government Task Force Report: Coping With Terror and Civil Disorders* (Washington, D.C.: U.S. Government Printing Office, 1987), p. 3.
52. Laqueur, *The Age of Terrorism*, p. 123.
53. Bush, *Public Report*, pp. 19–20.
54. Laqueur, p. 123.
55. Schreiber, *The Ultimate Weapon*, pp. 116–117.
56. Bush, pp. 19–20.
57. *Ibid.*
58. Moorehead, pp. 240–241.
59. "Reagan's Hostage Crisis," *U.S. News & World Report* (July 1, 1985), pp. 18–20.
60. "The Problems With Retaliation," *Time* (July 8, 1985), p. 20.
61. "The Search for a U.S. Anti-Terror Policy," *U.S. News & World Report* (October 21, 1985), pp. 29–30.
62. "Raid on Libya," *Time* (April 28, 1987), p. 23.
63. *Ibid.*
64. "Iran Plays the Hostage Game," *Newsweek* (February 9, 1987).
65. *Ibid.*, p. 34–36.
66. "Poindexter Never Told President of Contra Diversion," *Washington Post* (July 16, 1987), p. A15.
67. "Bush Told U.S. of Arms Deal," *Washington Post* (February 8, 1987), p. 1.
68. "Iran Plays the Hostage Game," *Newsweek*, pp. 34–36.
69. "Hostages: Living in the Aftermath," *U.S. News & World Report*, p. 34.
70. "Terrorism—How the West Can Win," *Reader's Digest*, pp. 110–115.
71. "Should the U.S. Strike Back at Terrorists?" *U.S. News & World Report* (April 14, 1986), p. 22.
72. "The Problem With Retaliation," *Time*, p. 20.
73. Adams, *The Financing of Terror*, p. 36.
74. Bush, *Public Report*, p. 12.
75. Bremer, *Counterterrorism: U.S. Policy and Proposed Legislation*, p. 45.
76. *Ibid.*, p. 47.
77. *Ibid.*, pp. 44–49.

BIBLIOGRAPHY

BOOKS

Adams, James. *The Financing of Terror*. New York: Simon & Schuster, 1987.

Bakhash, Shaul. *Iran and the Islamic Revolution*. New York: Basic Books, 1984.

Hubbard, David. *Winning Back the Sky*. Dallas: Saybrook Publishers, 1979.

Laqueur, Walter. *The Age of Terrorism*. New York: Little, Brown, 1987.

Meltzer, Milton. *The Terrorists*. New York: Harper & Row, 1983.

Moorehead, Caroline. *Hostages to Fortune*. New York: Atheneum, 1980.

Netanyahu, Benjamin. *Terrorism—How the West Can Win*. New York: Farrar, Straus, and Giroux, 1986.

Schreiber, William. *The Ultimate Weapon: Terrorists and World Order*. New York: William Morrow & Co., 1978.

Sickmann, Rocky. *Iranian Hostage—A Personal History*. North Carolina: Crawford Press, 1982.

Sterling, Claire. *The Terror Network*. Boston: Holt Rinehart & Winston, 1981.

Taylor, L. B. *Emergency Squads*. New York: Franklin Watts, 1980.

MAGAZINE ARTICLES

Newsweek
"Businessmen and Terrorism" (November 14, 1977), pp. 82–84.
"The Countdown in Uganda" (July 12, 1976), pp. 28–29.
"The Delicate Art of Handling Terrorists" (March 21, 1977), pp. 25–27.
"How the Israelis Pulled It Off" (July 19, 1976), pp. 42–46.
"Iran Plays the Hostage Game" (February 9, 1987), pp. 34–36.
"Seizing Hostages, Scourge of the '70s" (March 21, 1977), pp. 34–36.
"You Can Run, But You Can't Hide" (October 21, 1985), pp. 22–30.

Reader's Digest
"Kidnapped in Beirut" (April 1988), pp. 90–97.
"Terrorism—How the West Can Win" (July 1986), pp. 122–128.

Time
"Children in a School of Terror" (June 6, 1977), p. 39.
"The Hostage Dilemma" (October 20, 1975), p. 50.
"Hostage Release" (August 10, 1986), pp. 16–18.
"Horror and Death at the Olympics" (September 18, 1972), pp. 22–27.
"Lindbergh Nightmare" (February 5, 1973), p. 42.
"Murder on the Milk Train" (December 15, 1975), p. 25.
"The Problems With Retaliation" (July 8, 1985), p. 20.
"Raid on Libya" (April 28, 1987), p. 23.
"Rescuing Hostages: To Deal or Not to Deal" (September 18, 1972), pp. 30–31.
"Siege in Holland" (December 22, 1975), p. 32.
"Surrender in Amsterdam" (December 29, 1975), p. 25.
"The U.S. Sends a Message" (October 21, 1985), pp. 22–25.

U.S. News & World Report
"A Cry From the 'Other' Hostages" (September 29, 1986), p. 12.
"Hostages: Living in the Aftermath" (July 8, 1985), p. 34.
"Hostage Negotiator Who Stands Tall" (November 25, 1985), p. 13.
"Mideast Terror Strikes Americans" (June 24, 1985), p. 9.
"POW Swap Stirs Storm in Israel's War on Terrorists" (June 3, 1985), pp. 31–32.
"Reagan's Hostage Crisis" (July 1, 1985), pp. 18–20.
"Shultz Talks Tough on Terrorism" (October 25, 1984), p. 28.
"The Search for a U.S. Anti-Terror Policy" (October 21, 1985), pp. 29–30.
"Should the U.S. Strike Back at Terrorists?" (April 14, 1986), p. 22.

NEWSPAPERS

"American Journalist Abducted," *Newport News Daily Press.* Associated Press dispatch (June 19, 1987), p. 1.

"Bankrolling International Murder and Extortion," *Washington Post* (February 8, 1987), Bookweek Section, p. 3.

"Bush Told U.S. of Arms Deal," *Washington Post* (February 8, 1987), p. 1.

"Hostage Offer Refused," *Newport News Daily Press.* Associated Press dispatch (June 22, 1987), p. 1.

"Iran Deal 'A Mistake' Reagan Says," *Newport News Daily Press.* Associated Press dispatch (March 6, 1987), p. 1.

"Kidnappers Renew Threat to Kill Hostage," *Newport News Daily Press.* Associated Press dispatch (March 25, 1987), p. 1.

"Kidnappings More Likely McFarlane Says," *Newport News Daily Press.* Associated Press dispatch (June 6, 1987), p. 1.

"McFarlane Tells Reagan's Contra Role," *Virginia Pilot.* Los Angeles Times News Service (May 12, 1987), p. 1.

"Moscow's Invisible War of Terror Inside Pakistan," *Washington Post* (March 13, 1988), pp. C1–C4.

"My Hostage Life in Beirut Was Waiting and Praying," *Washington Post* (March 7, 1987), p. B1.

"Poindexter Never Told President of Contra Diversion," *Washington Post* (July 16, 1987), p. A15.

"President Rebuked in Iran-Contra Deal," *Newport News Daily Press.* Associated Press dispatch (February 27, 1987), p. 1.

"Rescue at Entebbe," *The New York Times* (July 11, 1976), p. 1.

"Syrians Vow to Win Release of Americans," *Newport News Daily Press* (June 23, 1987), p. 1.

"U.S. Hostages Taken to Iran," *Washington Post* (June 14, 1987), p. A-1.

SPECIAL REPORTS

Bremer, Paul. *Counterterrorism: U.S. Policy and Proposed Legislation.* Washington, D.C.: U.S. Department of State Bulletin, January 1988.

Bush, George. *Public Report of the Vice President: Task Force on Combatting Terrorism.* Washington, D.C.: U.S. Government Printing Office, 1986.

U.S. Government Task Force Report: Coping with Terror and Civil Disorders (Washington, D.C.: U.S. Government Printing Office, 1987), p. 3.

INDEX